DO MORE
MORE NATURALLY

**Empowering Effortless Success
and the Freedom to Be Yourself**

DO MORE
MORE NATURALLY

Empowering Effortless Success and the Freedom to Be Yourself

DAVID KOLBE AND AMY BRUSKE

IE

ethos
collective

Printed in the United States of America

Published by Igniting Souls
PO Box 43, Powell, OH 43065
IgnitingSouls.com

LCCN: 2024912322
Paperback ISBN: 978-1-63680-337-1
Hardcover ISBN: 978-1-63680-338-8
e-Book ISBN: 978-1-63680-339-5

Available in paperback, hardcover, e-book, and audiobook.

Any Internet addresses (websites, blogs, etc.) and telephone numbers printed in this book are offered as a resource. They are not intended in any way to be or imply an endorsement by Igniting Souls, nor does Igniting Souls vouch for the content of these sites and numbers for the life of this book.

Some names and identifying details may have been changed to protect the privacy of individuals.

The following terms are trademarks owned by Kathy Kolbe or Kolbe Corp:

Kolbe A™ Index, Kolbe B™ Index, Kolbe C™ Index, Kolbe Comparisons: A to A™, Kolbe Comparisons: A to B™, Kolbe Comparisons: A to C™, Role Alignment Guide™, Kolbe Coaching Report™, Kolbe TeamSuccess® Solutions, 12 Kolbe Strengths™, Action Modes®, Kolbe RightFit™, Kolbe Range of Success™, Kolbe Certified™, Takes Two®, Activate Your A™, Kolbe Youth™ Index, Student Aptitude™ Quiz

Third-Party Trademarks:

Strategic Coach® and Unique Ability® are registered trademarks of Strategic Coach, used with permission. EOS® and LMA® are registered trademarks of EOS Worldwide, LLC, used with permission.

Table of Contents

PART THREE: COLLABORATION

Chapter One
Why It Matters

"I wish I'd known about this sooner."

We hear that too often, and it's heartbreaking to have the secret that will help people to Do More without needless pain, stress, and frustration. On the one hand, it's gratifying that we make such a difference in people's lives. On the other, we hate hearing we could have helped them avoid years of pain, stress, and frustration but didn't get the message to them quickly enough.

We've been blessed to help millions of people achieve this mind shift, but there are so many more who don't know our secret. When you're done with this book, you'll have learned about the part of you that drives how you instinctively take action, and you'll know how to channel that energy to achieve the things you care about most.

Amy's Story

I still remember the day Kathy Kolbe challenged everything I'd ever considered about success. At the time, my salary was higher than almost anyone my age; I'd had five promotions and moved around the country because of them. Few in their late twenties had risen as high on the corporate ladder as I had. So, when she asked, "Amy, how do you define success?" I was taken completely off guard. "Your life looks pretty successful," she continued, "but I just wondered if your accomplishments fit your definition of success."

To be honest, I thought it was the strangest question I'd ever heard. I had no idea how to respond. Didn't everyone define success the same way? You graduate from college, find a lucrative career, and keep excelling until you retire. Right?

After a few seconds, Kathy broke the stunned silence. "Well, my definition of success is the freedom to be yourself."

Her words hit me like a lightning bolt. I believed I had found the path to success with a job that matched my skill set. But I was miserable. My role was a complete mismatch for my strengths, and I left work each day completely drained with no energy left to enjoy other parts of life outside of work. I thought the pain I felt was just part of life. I never dreamt people actually had freedom in their careers to work in a way that comes naturally. True joy and contentment were reserved for retirement. I'd get there someday. Working hard and swimming upstream were the norm. At least, that's how it looked to me.

That moment changed everything for me. I was clearly in a situation where I was not free to be myself, and I started to understand I couldn't build my success by changing who I really was. So, I did one of the most successful things I've ever done: I quit my job! This allowed me to begin a journey to discover my strengths and learn how to tap into them to get more done. Ultimately, I figured out how to find the right role for me, and I stopped feeling guilty about the tasks that made me miserable. Basic decisions became easier, higher performance felt effortless, and I began to feel more joy at work.

Every day, I encounter people living with the pain of working outside their natural strengths. It's like they're ants trying to push boulders up the hill. I know they have the same performance-at-all-costs mindset I had before Kathy talked to me that day. They don't even know there's a better way.

Our mission is to help people discover the joy of accomplishment and to thrive in what they do best. Only you can decide what's most important to you, but regardless of your priorities, we will give you a framework, and practical advice for achieving them.

Unlike productivity gurus who glorify grind culture, we don't want to convince you to work harder or smarter. Rather, we want this book to help you see you have inherent, identifiable strengths that you can learn to use more effectively and leverage to achieve what matters most to you. And you don't need to be an expert or have any specialized training to benefit from our immediately actionable tips.

To be blunt, our approach isn't for everyone. Those who think the only path to success requires difficult and complicated solutions will probably think our approach is naïve. The same goes for those who think leadership means making others just follow orders.

This book will have the biggest impact on those who:

- Respect and value their own strengths
- Respect and value the strengths of others
- Are seeking more productivity with less pain

Far too often, we see people lose the joy of accomplishment and start to associate getting things done with painful drudgery. But we and countless others have discovered life doesn't have to be that way. Every person has instinctive strengths, and when we allow those behaviors to drive us, we can have freedom, purpose, and confidence to Do More, More Naturally.

This is why we are excited to carry on Kathy Kolbe's legacy. We're on a mission to help people uncover their natural strengths so they can achieve a superior level of productivity and high performance in an easier and more sustainable way.

Just as Kathy Kolbe did that for Amy, it's what we want to do for you. Today's the day to redefine success and challenge yourself to Do More, More Naturally.

Have you taken your Kolbe A™ Index?

If so, write your numbers here so you can refer back to them as you read.

——— ——— ——— ———

Here are our results.

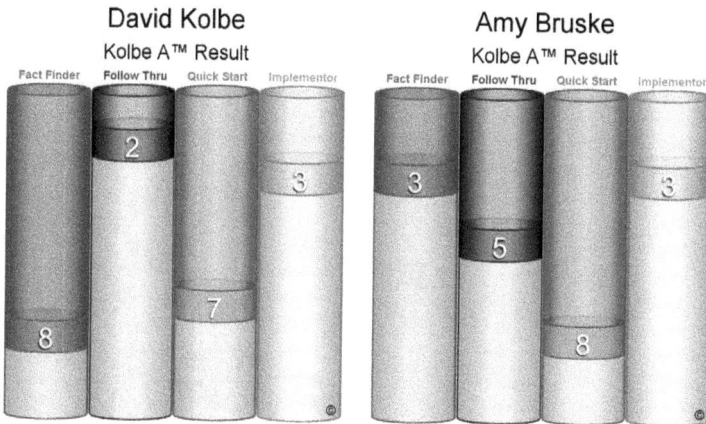

David Kolbe	Amy Bruske
Kolbe A™ Result	Kolbe A™ Result
Fact Finder Follow Thru Quick Start Implementor	Fact Finder Follow Thru Quick Start Implementor
8 2 7 3	3 5 8 3

More on what these numbers mean in Chapter Three.

Chapter Two
Effortless Success

What if we told you we know the secret to being extremely productive while living a full life—accomplishing more and leaving work exhilarated? Better still, how would you feel if you uncovered the mystery behind finding joy in accomplishment? There are times when all of us have been able to tap into something deep inside that seems to unlock the free flow of energy. Times when we would devote ourselves so completely to something that hours felt like minutes. Times when we would be excited to take on a challenge because even getting the chance to succeed seemed to fuel us without burning us out.

Some haven't felt that energy since they were kids. They wonder if it was a fluke, even discounting their earlier accomplishment by telling themselves they didn't earn it, it came "too easy," or seemed to appear out of the blue. They start to think they're an "imposter." Nope, the kind of success that comes when you tap into your instinctive strengths isn't getting lucky; it's identifiable, repeatable, and expandable.

Why does that statement seem too good to be true? Because we don't properly understand what drove us when we experienced that kind of success. Often, we simply don't identify what went right and why.

Unfortunately, most people start planning their future believing work will be and perhaps should be, difficult and tedious. We reject this notion. Not because we're afraid of hard work or challenges but because we think the perfect way to challenge yourself is to set big goals, not set yourself up for failure. Achieving greatness is hard enough; you shouldn't make it harder to accomplish by ignoring your strengths.

As you begin this adventure to finding freedom, it's important to understand the truth regarding success.

Everyone needs to ask the question Kathy asked Amy, "How do you define success?" Some people believe success can only be achieved in the midst of fatigue and weariness; they wear their exhaustion and even misery as a badge of honor. Others look for success measured by the markers others have set. They may make great money but don't have the "right" degree, or it's not from the "right" school. These individuals think they got lucky or their contributions have less value than others. Sometimes, they discount their achievements because they didn't do it the "right" way.

Particularly frustrating for the team at Kolbe Corp is when we see people do great things but don't feel the sense of accomplishment they deserve because they didn't do it the way a parent, teacher, coach, or mentor told them to.

So, before we go any further, be honest with yourself. What does success mean to you? You might want to have a notebook handy for this question and various activities throughout the book.

Amy's Story

When I began to consider Kathy's question, I stopped trying to change who I was. I also came to realize that deep down, everyone longs for the freedom to be themselves. Prior to my conversation with Kathy, I would have called myself successful. Looking back, I wonder if I was on the road to a heart attack or anxiety. I know the stress of my job was taking its toll, but at the time, I thought exhaustion was the price of success.

Redefining Success

Imagine getting up every morning psyched to go to work. With each new project, you know exactly which coworkers to enlist to get things done, and as you work on the project, the collaborations you create make everything move quickly. Being in the zone ramps up the entire team's level of productivity, and you go home every evening with plenty of energy for your personal life. What would you do at the end of the day if you had energy to burn?

You might think we just described a pipe dream, but a dreamlike work environment is possible. This approach of tapping into instinctive strengths can help with parenting, marriage, and other relationships. By understanding each of their children's unique needs, parents can be better guides and advocates for them. Having a better sense of self and knowing what drives the way a romantic partner operates will also set the stage for more supportive and less stressful relationships. Living in rhythm with your instinctive strengths and understanding the instincts of others makes all our connections better.

A 2023 Gallup poll reported that only a third of Americans feel engaged at work.[1] Zippia surveyed 1,000 people and discovered at least half of the workforce don't like their jobs.[2] They cite a variety of reasons, but we know underlying many of them is the disengagement caused by the lack of freedom to be themselves.

The dictionary defines success as "a favorable or desired outcome." Many people have a certain number correlating to an accumulated wealth account or an annual income in mind. Still, the definition of success is subjective, and achieving it seems elusive.[3] What sacrifices do we make daily with our health and contentment to achieve this constantly morphing idea of success?

What if you, and all those who take action every day, began to use Kathy's definition of success? How would our lives look different if we embraced a new idea of freedom?

Breaking the Bias

Stop reading and take a minute to write your name with your non-dominant hand. Unless you're among the one percent who are ambidextrous, you'll struggle. Ask a lefty born before 1965 what it was like to be forced to learn to write with their right hand. Believe it or not, it was common practice to punish a child who picked up a pencil with their left hand. Many still have poor handwriting as a result. By the final third of the twentieth century, most schools understood children are born left- or right-handed, and trying to train them to write with their non-dominant hand wasn't very productive.

You would never waste time learning to write legibly with your non-dominant hand. You also don't consider yourself unsuccessful because you are not ambidextrous. Why, then, do we try to force ourselves into conventional molds when it comes to the way we carry out tasks? We set ourselves up for failure and then beat ourselves up when we can't do the work as fast or efficiently as Bob or Grace. Just like our handedness, some things about us are innate and unchanging. When we feel like a failure because we're working outside our natural ability, it's as if we're defining success as learning how to write perfectly with our non-dominant hand.

Parents and teachers have the best of intentions when they try to retrain the children in their care. How many times in your youth did you hear, "There's a right way to do everything"? In school, they taught us to write reports using specific steps—first you create the outline, then do the research, then write the paper. But nearly everyone had a friend who skipped the index cards or the outline and aced the assignment.

David's Story

One of my kids showed an early interest and talent in math. Both in and outside of school, he sought ways to explore the subject. He naturally learned the concepts and rules, then experimented by applying them in ways different than he'd been taught. Sometimes, it worked; other times, it didn't. Either way, the process fascinated him.

His love of numbers continued to grow until he had a teacher who insisted her students not only understand the concepts she taught, but also apply them using her method only. It wasn't enough to show your work and get the correct answer. If students got the right answer but their work showed a method other than hers, she marked it wrong—even if they had previously demonstrated they understood her method and even if the child's method proved to be a more advanced way to get to the correct answer.

As you might imagine, this did not go over well with an 11-year-old. It felt wrong, unfair, and punitive. This teacher's method of instruction managed to squash my son's interest in math. When he got to do it in a way that was natural for him, he enjoyed it. But when he was forced to use math in a way counter to his natural approach, the subject became dull and he lost his drive.

The experience didn't make him less smart about math. (Albert Einstein himself famously left school at the age of 15 due, at least in part, to rigid school curriculum!) My son easily completed the work, and he learned to play the game so he could receive a good grade. But he no longer wanted to do math outside of school. As he continued in his education, he took advanced classes in math and excelled in them because they played a role in his larger academic goals. Still, he never again pursued the subject outside of school or considered careers that relied heavily on math skills. The idea of doing math beyond what was required was now torture.

The thing is, in almost all other respects, this woman was a great teacher. She cared about her students and put in extra hours to help those who lagged behind, as well as the ones with high potential whose approach matched her own. She knew her subject well, and students who naturally approached math her way thrived.

Stories like this, where talented people are pushed in the wrong direction by well-meaning people, happen in schools, families, and workplaces too often. We hope you'll have the clarity and confidence to pursue your own path using your strengths rather than letting others push you away from them. We also hope you'll understand that just because how you operate works for you, it isn't going to be best for everyone.

We all have some level of bias on how best to accomplish a task. Everyone has done it. Someone says, "I need to get more organized." Another wishes they could finish a project without getting so distracted. And those who excel at being organized or working with their hands often add to the guilt of those who don't by imposing their own methods on them. We do it to our children and co-workers every day. We don't mean to. But because our way of doing something comes so easily, we assume everyone should be able to achieve the same outcome in the same way. Without an awareness of the diverse ways that people naturally solve problems, we'll tend to be frustrated with people who complete tasks differently than we do.

Amy's Story

Growing up, I got straight A's and took honor classes. Still, I felt dumb. My dad and mom attended Berkeley and Stanford, and both always seemed to have detailed information to back up every point they made. At the dinner table, when the discussion invited my input, my family would ask me to justify my thoughts or provide data to reinforce my opinion. After a while, I just quit talking. I can look back now and understand why I felt so different from the others in my family. I am a natural simplifier, and I don't have the same need or natural drive to delve into the details as they do. The insight into why I never felt a need to defend my position with external facts allowed me to just let it go.

I wasn't the only one in my family to feel "less than" because of the way someone influential reacted to the way they did things. My grandfather was a copper miner who excelled when working with his hands. Nearly every time he visited, my dad ended up feeling as though he couldn't do anything right. My grandfather was also a natural planner who saw projects through to completion. He immediately noticed all the things my dad had jury-rigged or left undone. My grandfather meant well, but with each critique, my dad felt like a failure. Dad looked at those projects from the perspective of "it works—it opens; it closes; it's fine." My grandfather wanted to help my dad ensure his work would stand the test of time. Their natural ways of solving problems fell on opposite ends of the continuum.

At Kolbe, we strive to help people understand the fact they have natural innate strengths—instinctive ways to execute—and break the bias associated with doing things the "right way." As people develop an appreciation for the variety of ways the strengths work together and start to focus on excellent results rather than how work gets done, they'll experience increased productivity, freedom, and joy. Understanding these instincts sets people free to achieve the goal and stop fretting about how they get there.

This idea of instinctive strengths confirms a lesson couples often figure out the hard way—you cannot change how a person is hard-wired to take action. The part of your mind that drives the way you work is a stable trait. When anyone on our team gives a presentation and mentions the reality that you can't change your partner, laughter fills the room. Nearly everyone who has been in a relationship long enough has attempted to retrain the other person. Whether it's a spouse, partner, close friend, or coworker, we've all asked someone to take on a task and then felt the need to tell them how to do it better. The beauty of understanding these innate strengths is coming to the realization that it's not about fixing your partner; it's about finding ways for the two of you to use your strengths. That leads to less conflict and more harmony.

What Does Do More, More Naturally Really Mean?

If you are like many of our clients, you have either read a book, listened to a podcast, or attended a training about increasing productivity. Some may have centered on mindset or habits. Others have a system for time management or how to handle your email. These programs focus entirely on **doing more**. While a few tips they offered probably helped you in the short term, there is a good chance most faded quickly or didn't work for you. Almost anyone can try out a new system and achieve improved performance for a short while, but sustainable high-level performance is much harder to achieve. Unfortunately, applying most well-meaning advice will only work if you can execute it in alignment with your natural way of taking action. This is the **More Naturally** part of the picture.

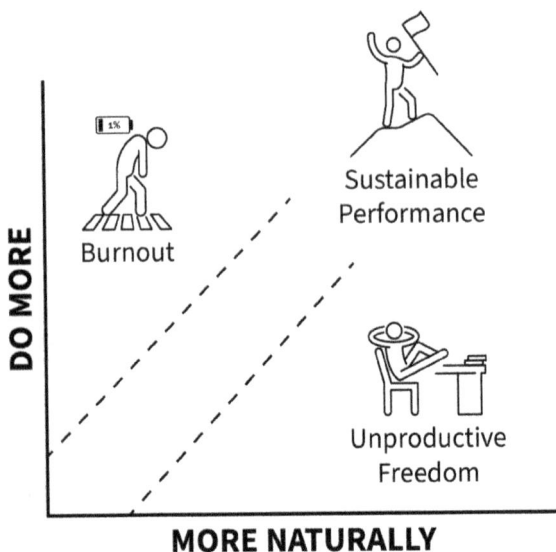

What do we mean by Doing More? It is not just doing more for the sake of more. It's taking action on more of what helps you reach your goals, more of what gets results, and more of what matters to you most. You must take responsibility for choosing to do the right things that will achieve the necessary outcomes. Doing things More Naturally means using your unique, instinctive strengths. We all have a certain amount of mental energy available to solve problems, make decisions, and execute. Discovering and effectively tapping into this energy source is what leads to people feeling they are in a "flow state" where work feels more effortless.

Trying to do more but in a way that doesn't fit your strengths results in using significantly more energy without achieving the highest quality results. Also, even when trying to do very little, if you're doing it less naturally, it will still be awkward, stressful, and annoying. Doing little but more naturally may start to feel like a pleasant, relaxing vacation, but isn't productive. Finally, when operating more naturally, you'll be able to do more and achieve better results while using less energy and experiencing less stress. That's the sweet spot of sustainable success.

Understanding the Three C's

After working with clients to align their actions with their instinctive strengths, we've found there are three main things to master. We call this framework the Three C's of Sustainable Performance.

- Clarity
- Commitment
- Collaboration

Many wonder why some people seem so much less productive than others. They blame it on a lack of motivation, abilities, IQ, and more. However, Kathy Kolbe's investigation into a millennia-old theory revealed these low-performance individuals simply lack these Three C's of Performance—Clarity, Commitment, and Collaboration.

When someone doesn't understand their instincts and the way they operate, it's hard for them to achieve repeatable and sustainable success. Fortunately, this can be easily addressed, whether by taking a Kolbe A Index or using a process of reflecting on and analyzing what has driven their success in the past. When people discover their innate strengths, they develop the first C. Clarity allows them to see why they feel empowered in some situations and like a fish out of water in others. When the light bulb turns on, they begin to see endless possibilities.

Many who wear glasses remember the first time they looked through their corrective lenses. More than one young person has walked out of the optician's office and looked at a tree as if they'd never seen one before. Prior to glasses, trees looked like big green clouds. With the new lenses, every individual leaf becomes clear. It is as if a veil lifts, revealing the beauty of everything around them. In the same way, discovering innate strengths is a liberating event. Suddenly, the parts of your life that looked cloudy because you compared yourself to everyone else makes sense. Every person on the Kolbe team looks forward to interacting with people as they experience the excitement, validation, relief, and sometimes—we aren't exaggerating—tears of joy that accompany this new understanding of themselves.

Becoming aware of why you naturally solve problems the way you do is just the beginning. You also need to know how to commit your energy effectively and make wise choices every day on what deserves your best efforts. Clarity without Commitment robs you of reaching your highest level of performance as well as the potential to find freedom and joy in your work. You have to break through your own and others' biases to truly commit your mental energy in productive ways, but the abundant reward more than makes up for the effort.

We find people constantly amazed at the increase in quality of life after they commit to understanding and working within their instinctive strengths. However, the reality of highest performance comes when we learn to Collaborate strategically. The spot where Clarity, Commitment, and Collaboration meet endows us with productivity, power, and peace we never imagined possible.

The Three C's in Action

Our friend and colleague Dan Sullivan, who co-founded Strategic Coach® with his wife, Babs Smith, is a great example of someone who knows the importance of mastering Clarity, Commitment, and Collaboration to achieve astounding results.

Dan is smart. In fact, he's proven to be brilliant at coaching people and developing programs and content to help them successfully lead businesses and shape the lives they desire. This knack became apparent to him early in his career, as did his desire to start his own business.

When Dan launched his business, he prepared himself for hard work and long hours. A rugged individualist, he was doing everything himself, resulting in an unsustainable situation that led to bankruptcy. But three years later, he met Babs Smith, a fellow business owner who recognized Dan's unique gifts—gifts she wanted to share with the world.

Without Clarity around his strengths, Dan was struggling. But when Babs looked at his activities and saw that he was doing everything in his business himself, she asked him, "Why are you doing that? Let's get somebody else to do that." As they peeled away the tasks that didn't involve Dan's strengths and talents, they built a team around them of other uniquely capable people to take on those tasks and founded a new business together called Strategic Coach.

The process of identifying what Dan was best at and delegating the rest led to the development of the concept of Unique Ability®—what you love to do and do best. This became the backbone of Dan and Bab's business, with Unique Ability Teamwork becoming the framework in which everyone on the team operates within their own area of Unique Ability.

Dan describes two keys for gaining Clarity—his concept of Unique Ability and his Kolbe A Index results. In 1990, Dan and Babs were introduced to the Kolbe A Index, which took their clarity to another level. They had a team of five people who all took it, and it was a revelation.

The first step in achieving such a transformation is understanding excellence isn't determined by how smart we are or by what we've been trained to do. It's also about having the right instinctive strengths to complete the task. As Dan puts it, "The day I got my results back was one of the most liberating days of my life. I could just see everything: where I got into trouble, where I got frustrated, what stressed me out. Getting my Kolbe numbers (Kolbe A result) gave me an incredible blueprint that explained how I could have very energizing, very productive days instead. It let me focus on the new products and new experiences we would create."

Dan Sullivan
Kolbe A™ Result

Fact Finder	Follow Thru	Quick Start	Implementor
2	2		4
		10	

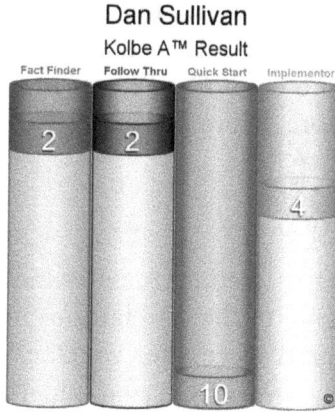

Clarity was crucial, but knowing how to Commit his energy pushed him even further. In addition to knowing his strengths, he developed strategies to let him focus on the tasks that fell within his Unique Abilities and not be sucked into unproductive roles. One of these is Strategic Coach's The 4 C's Formula®, a process that focuses on Commitment, Courage, Capability, and Confidence to help people achieve a bigger future.

But for Dan and almost everyone else, the ability to wisely commit your energy requires collaborating with others, as Dan's collaboration with Babs proved. With a brilliance that matched Dan's while possessing different strengths, Babs was crucial to building a team of smart, creative, and driven people who gave Dan the space to work in his Unique Ability while using their own instinctive strengths and areas of Unique Ability to do the other things the business needed.

Mastering Collaboration was indispensable in allowing Dan to have the freedom to be himself, which has driven his success and the success of his business and coaching clients.

In the following pages, we want to introduce you to the instinctive part of your mind and unlock the potential found there for those who commit to exploring the possibilities when they Do More, More Naturally.

Key Takeaways

1. Success is the freedom to be yourself. It's not about measuring up to the standards of others. How have you measured success for yourself?

2. The Three C's of Sustainable Performance are Clarity, Commitment, and Collaboration.

3. Discovering your instinctive strengths is the first key to getting Clarity and knowing what to Commit to.

PART ONE
Clarity

To know thyself is the beginning of wisdom.
—Socrates

Chapter Three

The Three Dimensions of the Mind

To "Know Thyself" is both ancient wisdom and modern obsession. Since the advent of psychological assessments in the late 1800s, people have been fascinated with analyzing and assessing our thought processes and intelligence levels in various ways. Then, as the therapeutic age began in the early 1900s, and we began to better understand human psychological types, we started to move our focus toward "personality."

It makes sense to spend our collective mental energy assessing, measuring, and considering how we think and feel and how those things affect the way we live in the world. Those two factors, the thinking—cognitive—part of the mind and the feeling—affective—part of the mind are hugely important. You can't really have clarity about who you are if you don't understand the way you think and feel.

The cognitive part of the mind speaks to our reasoning and intelligence. Your ability to gain knowledge is determined by your cognitive capacity. Each time you learn new information or gain a new skill, the thinking part of your mind changes and develops. The thinking part of the mind tells the world what you can do.

The affective part of your mind is associated with feelings and values, likes and dislikes. Your personality is rooted in the affective. This part of the mind determines what motivates you as well as what you prefer to do. It answers the question, "What do you want to do?"

We like knowing how smart we are and how our emotions and personalities drive us to interact with others. Interestingly enough, both of these parts of your mind can be improved, developed, and changed. We know that we can continuously develop our cognitive abilities by learning and acquiring new skills. Most of us have witnessed personality changes when our friends have suffered tremendous grief or amazing amounts of encouragement.

Intelligence and personality tests are commonplace. Magazines feature them; games on your devices tease you into playing by telling you they can measure your IQ. While these might be fun to do, the information they provide is often not helpful in making career decisions or learning how to be more productive. And while this information has value, the cognitive and affective parts of your mind alone aren't the sole predictors of long-term success.

There's a third, less well-known part of the mind which has been overlooked for a couple of centuries. This is the conative part of the mind. It drives the way you take action, and it is an indispensable part of knowing how you operate at work and at home.

Think back to a time when you had a really important decision to make. You thought about all the ways other people would handle it. Then, you considered everything you'd been taught to do in a similar situation. Regardless of how much you contemplated those methods, you had this gut feeling that you should approach the problem in a different way. How many times was the best decision the gut feeling?

Most of the time when we ask a similar question to a group, they'll say the gut decision produced the best results. Despite this experience, we can feel torn. Often, our learned behavior masks what we know deep down is the best approach for us.

All this stems from never having been told much about the conative part of the mind, the part that drives the way you take action. But these conative strengths are what we should get excited about. This part of your mind gives you your unique edge. While the cognitive part of the mind determines what you CAN do, and the affective reveals what you WANT to do, the conative controls HOW you can best get it done. We often define them as the thinking, feeling, and doing parts of the mind.

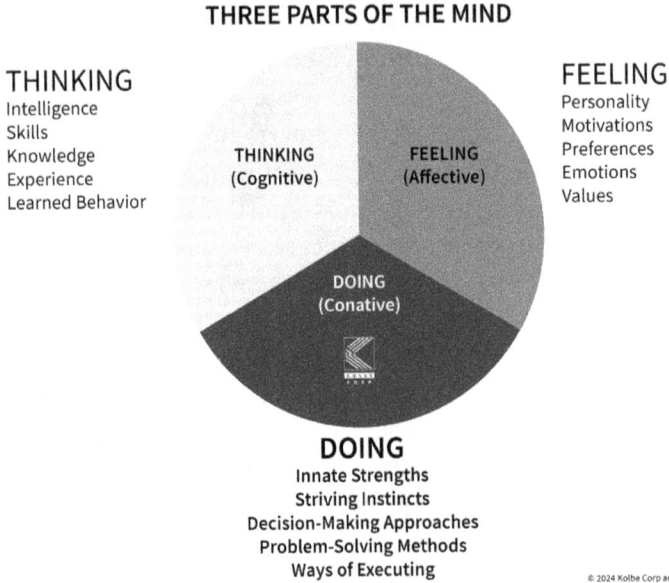

THREE PARTS OF THE MIND

THINKING
Intelligence
Skills
Knowledge
Experience
Learned Behavior

FEELING
Personality
Motivations
Preferences
Emotions
Values

THINKING
(Cognitive)

FEELING
(Affective)

DOING
(Conative)

DOING
Innate Strengths
Striving Instincts
Decision-Making Approaches
Problem-Solving Methods
Ways of Executing

© 2024 Kolbe Corp and Kathy Kolbe

Conation (pronounced like ice cream cone) drives the actions you most naturally use to solve problems, your striving instincts. This part of the mind doesn't require education or training because it's how you innately do things most effectively. It's who you have been since birth. However, these instincts only kick in when you're purposefully engaged and taking action, not when you're just performing tasks out of habit or learned behavior. When we tap into those instincts, life is just easier. We're more decisive, our relationships are healthier, and our career choices are clearer.

Just like glasses give near-sighted people more clarity and confidence, understanding conation can do the same for you.

We believe the conative part of the mind is the missing puzzle piece in human performance. When we add the conative dimension to personality and intelligence factors, we can see more clearly how you think, how you feel, and how you best get things done. In order to be free to be yourself, you need to maximize the potential of all three of your mental factors.

The Way You Think

The cognitive part of the mind represents your intelligence and skills. It's built by experience and education. Your cognitive abilities transform with every book you read and every new activity you attempt. Think about it as all the things you would include on your resume. If you list everything you have the ability to do, including your learned behavior, habits, and the knowledge you've acquired, you'll have a description of your cognitive strengths and practical intelligence.

Many tests help measure these cognitive capabilities. They tell us how well someone can use information and logic to answer questions or make educated guesses. Most jobs require some baseline level of mental capacity to complete tasks (you probably don't want to be represented by a lawyer who can't pass the bar exam or, worse yet, be served by a barista who can't get your "special" coffee order right). Unfortunately, employers often place so much emphasis on getting the best and brightest in the room that they miss other vital pieces of the puzzle. Human resources departments concentrate on intelligence and schooling, yet there is very little correlation between someone's IQ test scores or education and their ability to be a productive team member.

Granted, some professions need a higher level of education and skills. We want our medical professionals to have the appropriate degrees. But when we place the highest importance on this part of the mind, we cheat ourselves out of some of the most qualified candidates.

We've even made that mistake at Kolbe Corp. One applicant especially impressed us with their cognitive credentials. After graduating with honors from a rigorous Ivy League program, the candidate scored very well on an intelligence test we gave as part of our screening process. And it wasn't just "on-paper" intelligence. We watched this person solve discrete problems that were presented to them. They reviewed the relevant information, drew good conclusions, and presented logical solutions.

Unfortunately, this position needed a different kind of smarts. The person we hired was great at taking an identified complex problem and coming up with a specific solution using lots of available data, but the job was much more open-ended than that. It needed someone who was good at figuring out what required immediate attention and how to get relevant information that wasn't already being collected. It was about figuring out what information to collect, making decisions about which problems and opportunities should be the top priority, and deciding which people on our team would be best at doing that work. We trained them on our processes and gave them time to learn about the people they supervised, but they never got good at the most critical parts of the job. The bottom line was that their cognitive abilities weren't the right ones for success in the role.

So, while the person we hired was very smart, they weren't able to find and focus on the most important issues to achieve the results we needed. They didn't have the right kind of smarts for that job.

We've also seen many of the classic, almost stereotypical examples of people who come in with all the intelligence they need to succeed, only to have personality problems that lead to their failure. For instance, the genius whose arrogance causes them to ignore and discount other's contributions or the leader who is so demanding that they create a culture of fear. And while cognitive disconnects may seem to be the most detrimental, ignoring affective issues has similar results.

Personality, Preferences, Values

During World War I, the Army started using personality testing in an attempt to predict which soldiers would suffer "shellshock"—better known as PTSD today. Though the war ended before they could determine their usefulness, those personality tests laid the groundwork for what has become a multi-million dollar industry.

During the middle of the twentieth century, the Myers-Briggs Type Indicator® became one of the earliest assessments to measure how people perceive and judge things and whether they are an introvert or extrovert.[4] Soon after, employers began to use affective assessments like the DiSC Behavior Inventory® or Hogan Personality Inventory™ to see if potential candidates would make good hires.

The affective part of the mind reflects your motivations and preferences. It's the seat of our emotions. Probably one of the most influential pieces of information we gain from this part of the mind is a person's values. In business, as in most other parts of life, having values that align with the people around you is critical to success. Prominent business experts like Gino Wickman, founder of The Entrepreneurial Operating System (EOS®), and Patrick Lencioni provide models for making sure new team members share your company's core values. Even the smartest person with the right instincts for the job won't fit in your organization if they don't adopt your core values.

Like the cognitive, the affective part of your mind can be molded. Mindsets can be changed, and feelings contained. We usually adopt our parents' values as youth; however, media, higher education, and our passions can remake them as we grow older. As we learn more about people and situations, we rethink our perspective. Every relationship and experience shapes our desires and motivations.

Amy's Story

Personality tests have shown me that I have what some might call "perfectionist tendencies." Getting my CliftonStrengths® assessment result showed that I value transforming something strong into something superb. I now understand why, at the end of every meeting or project, I immediately look for what we could have done better. Knowing this about my personality helped me see I needed to start my debrief by focusing on what went well so I don't cause the rest of my team to feel frustrated or demoralized, implying that what we just finished wasn't good enough. And don't worry; I won't stop working on this until I get it just right!

Discovering personality and value differences during the hiring process can prevent tremendous upheaval in your organization later. Though these parts of our mind can be remolded to some extent, if someone has values completely opposite of everyone else in your company, finding balance will be impossible. Likewise, that person who always leads and can never be a follower has the potential to be a great entrepreneur, but they might not be cut out for a team atmosphere.

How You Need to Take Action

At Kolbe Corp, we recognize the vital nature of cognitive and affective strengths; however, our specialty is the third part of the mind, the *conative*—the part too many people dismiss. Since Plato and Aristotle first mentioned this aspect of mental processes and its connection to a person's actions, the idea of conation has come in and out of vogue. At the end of the 1800s, William James argued humans could work as effortlessly and automatically as insects and animals. While other scientists believed men and women take action because of their ability to reason, James sensed we had a natural instinct, much like the animals. He said our more developed minds have greater instincts, but we humans take those instincts for granted because they work so well.

William McDougall, G.F. Stout, Kurt Goldstein, Sigmund Freud, and others continued the conversation in the 1900s. They realized each person had something deep inside driving their behaviors. The way humans instinctively act is more than just a rational response to situations. The conative part of the mind propels us into action.[5]

If things could be accomplished simply because of what we know or how we feel, everyone would be able to conquer New Year's resolutions with just a bit of knowledge or passion. But the third part of the mind adds the action to how we think and feel.

The conative part of the mind takes the way you feel and the knowledge you have acquired and drives the way you take action on what you can and want to do. Each person's instincts drive them to approach problems in distinct and different ways. We aren't referring to instincts like "fight or flight" or "maternal instincts," though. Rather, these are the innate, action-oriented ways each of us naturally gets things done. We use these instincts when we are striving and taking purposeful action.

A human's ability to choose when to put their instincts into action marks a major difference between animal and human instinctive behavior. This same ability lets us decide to work against our natural traits and make tasks a chore rather than a pleasure. Unfortunately, our advanced intelligence and ability to adapt have led many people to work outside their innate strengths and do it well, leaving them looking successful on the outside but feeling miserable on the inside.

David's Story

For me, the starkest example of a conative mismatch was my experience as a lawyer. Without knowing exactly why, I had wanted to be a lawyer since I was a little kid, so after a stint working in Congress, I headed to law school. I did well and was fortunate to land a job with an outstanding mid-size firm in my hometown of Phoenix. I was excited to join the firm, and it provided me with the additional on-the-job training necessary for any newly minted law school graduate to learn what it really takes to be a good lawyer.

The legal profession is a broad one with many different ways to get the job done. My assignment as a young associate put a heavy emphasis on following process and procedure, handling the logistics of projects, and following the successful templates the firm had created for its practice areas. And since we were paid based on our hours worked, I had to track my time in six-minute increments. Frankly, I wasn't a great fit for that role. I can focus on bringing things to closure, following established rules, and making sure all the "i's" get dotted and "t's" get crossed, but it's draining for me. This aspect made the practice of law, which I still have an intellectual attraction to, a grind.

Understanding my conative strengths made it easier for me to leave the law firm and join an entrepreneurial business with fewer rules and more opportunities to experiment. The fact Kolbe Corp would allow me to help craft a role to work with others with complementary strengths was also a plus. I could work in a way that was natural for me, and someone else would take care of necessary process-driven things that weren't a good fit for me.

Everyone is capable of problem solving and taking action, and our conative strengths determine how we instinctively get those things done. Unlike the cognitive and affective, conative abilities are unchanging and don't vary by gender, age, or race. Kathy Kolbe identified twelve conative strengths in four different modes. And she found a way to measure them. You can desire to work in one of the modes outside your strength. You can even become very adept at working

DO MORE, MORE NATURALLY

against them; however, at the end of the day, you'll feel completely drained.

Finding Your "Sweet Spot"

Each of the three dimensions of the mind is extremely important. You have strengths and unique traits in each one. At Kolbe, we find a lot of the testing done around intelligence and personality to be informative and helpful in understanding ourselves and the people we work with.

And while we don't want to discount the value of these more traditional indicators, they have been overemphasized. Overlooking the conative means we miss a huge piece of the puzzle. When we're able to use our strengths and abilities in all three parts of the mind, we move into our sweet spot. This allows us to take our preferences and execute in such a way we feel more productive and use the least amount of mental energy.

We've been taught for so long that there's a right way to do things, and it feels like we must be doing something wrong when we try to do things in a more natural way. It's easy to fall into the trap of working against your grain when society rewards you for working through pain versus doing what's natural and easy for you. Even when you understand your strengths in the conative part of the mind, it can still be incredibly difficult to trust these instincts.

One of the rules Kathy lives by is to *Act Before You Think*.[6] While this might sound irresponsible, it does not mean you should jump off a cliff without looking. Instead, it reminds us we miss opportunities to get our best results when our cognitive selves stop us from tapping into our instinctive way of getting things done. If you've ever been stuck overthinking a decision, you know what this feels like. Overthinking prevents us from making our best decisions, especially if we get other people's opinions too early in the process or let years of learned behavior keep us from taking action.

Once you become more aware of your strengths in all three parts of the mind, you can see when your natural instincts are being dominated by your learned behavior or what you value. If you trust in the cognitive part of your mind over all else, you miss out on tapping into the power of your instincts to fully engage in the creative process to solve problems.

In the Zone

To help people find their sweet spot, Kathy Kolbe created the Kolbe A Index. This assessment helps us discover our most natural way to solve problems. It has nothing to do with how smart you are or your personality type. It answers the question, "If I was free to do things in the most natural way possible, how would I approach this problem or project?"

The conative part of the mind operates in four instinct-based Action Modes®. We call them Fact Finder, Follow Thru, Quick Start, and Implementor. Each mode has its own continuum numbered from 1 to 10, with 1 at the top and 10 at the bottom. It's important to note that these aren't ratings or scores: a 1 is not better than a 10, and a 10 isn't better than a 1. These numbers provide a scale to identify the degree to which someone takes action in that particular mode.

Continuums of Behavior in Action Modes

Fact Finder	Follow Thru	Quick Start	Implementor
gathers and shares information	organizes and designs	deals with risk and uncertainty	handles space and tangibles
Simplify	Adapt	Stabilize	Envision

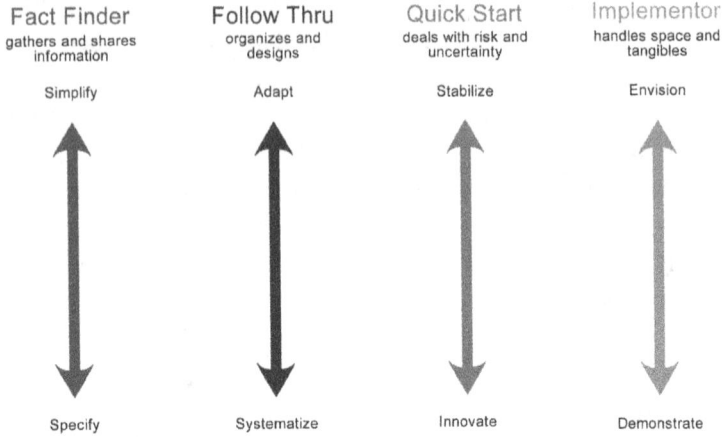

Specify	Systematize	Innovate	Demonstrate

© 1989-2024 Kathy Kolbe and Kolbe Corp. All rights reserved

Fact Finder: The instinctive way we gather and share information.

Behavior ranges from those who need to get as many facts as possible to those who just need an overview. And in the middle of the continuum are those who get and review essential facts.

Follow Thru: The instinctive way we organize and design.

This behavior ranges from those who will instinctively design systems to those whose organizational system looks more like piles to be adaptable. If someone has already designed a system, those in the middle will Accommodate it and make adjustments as necessary.

Quick Start: The instinctive way we deal with risk and uncertainty.

Behavior ranges from those who embrace change and need to experiment to those who need to create stability and minimize chaos. In the middle are people who bridge the gap to create sustainable change.

Implementor: *The instinctive way we handle space and tangibles.*
Behavior ranges from making things more concrete by building solutions to being more abstract by imagining a solution. In between are those who are great at repairing what's already there.

These Action Modes represent the ways we naturally solve problems, and each of the continuums is divided into three Zones of Operation.

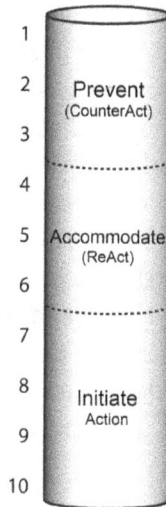

Zones of Operation

1	
2	Prevent
	(CounterAct)
3	
4	
5	Accommodate
	(ReAct)
6	
7	
8	Initiate
	Action
9	
10	

If you have a number in the 7–10 range of the continuum, you will use this mode to Initiate Action and begin the problem-solving process. This is where you will naturally spend most of your time and mental energy when you are free to be yourself.

If your strength lies in the 1–3 zone of the continuum, you will Prevent problems from occurring in that particular mode. Those with the longest lines in the mode immediately start taking the initiative, and those with the shortest lines use this mode to CounterAct or push back against letting those initiatives go too far. People who Initiate (7–10) in a mode need people who work in the 1–3 zone of that mode to provide balance. If we don't understand conative strengths, the people with a 7–10 may seem demanding, while those with a 1–3 will seem resistant, sometimes causing conflict between team members on the two ends of the continuum. They need people who bridge that gap.

Those whose numbers fall between 4-6 use this mode to Accommodate action or ReAct as needed in this area, building a bridge between those whose strengths fall on either end of the continuum. They can see both sides, and they Accommodate and respond to opportunities in that mode.

When you learn to leverage your strengths in all three parts of the mind, you will be more creative and experience the joy and fulfillment of true success. You've spent a good deal of your lives learning about and developing your cognitive and affective strengths. In order to Do More, More Naturally, you now need a deeper understanding of conative strengths and how all 12 Kolbe Strengths™ work together.

12 Kolbe Strengths™

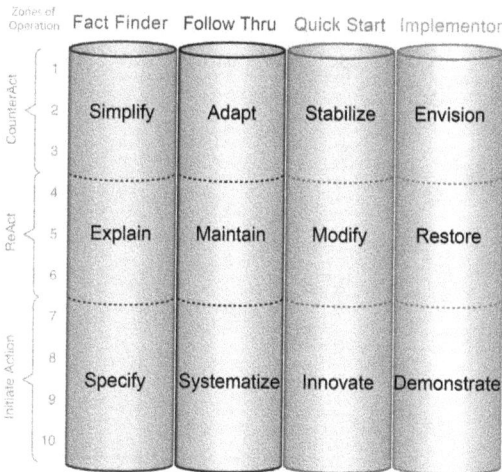

Zones of Operation	Fact Finder	Follow Thru	Quick Start	Implementor
CounterAct (1, 2, 3)	Simplify	Adapt	Stabilize	Envision
ReAct (4, 5, 6)	Explain	Maintain	Modify	Restore
Initiate Action (7, 8, 9, 10)	Specify	Systematize	Innovate	Demonstrate

Key Takeaways

1. It has long been recognized that there are three parts of your mind, each of which is distinct and important.

   - The cognitive part of your mind has to do with thinking and how smart you are.
   - The affective part of your mind is concerned with your feelings and personality type.
   - The conative part of your mind is responsible for how you solve problems, make decisions, and naturally take action. Unlike the cognitive and affective, research shows the conative part of the mind doesn't change over time.

2. The conative part of the mind operates in four instinct-based Action Modes: Fact Finder, Follow Thru, Quick Start, and Implementor.

3. Being free to use your conative strengths is directly tied to being "in the zone."

Chapter Four

Actions Speak Louder than Words

Our desire for self-awareness goes deeper than knowing how smart we are and what we're passionate about. As we just learned, to Do More, More Naturally, we must consider how our own conative strengths equip us to do the things that matter to us in a way that brings more fulfillment with less stress.

Everyone has a strength in each of the four Action Modes we just introduced. Now, we're going to go deeper to discuss how you actually get things done when you're in the zone. If you've already discovered your innate strengths by taking the Kolbe A Index, this can be a useful review and give you new insights into other people in your life.

Even if you haven't taken a Kolbe A Index, you probably have an intuitive sense of some of your strengths and your best ways of getting things done. When you review the following descriptions, consider which ones resonate with you as the types of actions you would naturally take. Sometimes, it's easier to identify what you would avoid doing. If it gives you a visceral reaction to even hear the description, it's probably something you would resist doing because it would be working against your natural instincts.

When you do take the Kolbe A, it will validate all four of your conative strengths and give you powerful language to use when describing them to others.

How Do You Gather and Share Information?

The first continuum in the Kolbe Index is called Fact Finder. It measures the way you gather and share information. Everyone takes in and passes on information every day. Whether it's a tidbit from social media, a major news story, or something new about your family, you've heard or shared some fun fact today.

Kolbe Action Modes

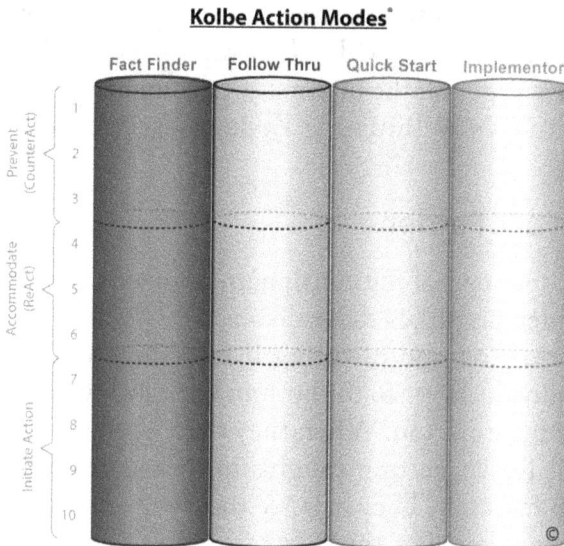

Fact Finder · Follow Thru · Quick Start · Implementor

7–10 in Fact Finder

An Initiating Fact Finder, someone whose number lies between a 7–10 on the continuum, accomplishes tasks by gathering as much available information as possible. They need to do in-depth research and will spend much of their time and mental energy doing so. For them, the more details, the better, so you'll need to give them a lot of specifics—or give them room to find them—before they move forward in a project.

The Initiating Fact Finder will justify their answers and back up their opinion with facts they've found. You can count on their answers to be precise and specific. They will strive to be an expert in the subjects they talk about.

People with this strength begin by getting all the data, including what has worked in the past. Then, they make decisions based on the information they gather as well as experience. Lawyers and accountants are often Initiating

Fact Finders. These professionals need the attention to detail this strength provides. If you're someone who checks four or five pages on the internet search engine, you probably fall into this 7–10 Initiating Zone of Fact Finder.

1–3 in Fact Finder

On the other end of the continuum, someone with a 1–3 in Fact Finder simplifies those details. They're great at taking the information and distilling it into three bullet points. These individuals get to the bottom line quickly and simplify complex information. When they're free to be themselves, they will Resist getting caught up in analyzing data and in-depth research. They balance those who Initiate in Fact Finder well, keeping them from getting bogged down in the details. Please don't ask them to justify their answers. Be prepared to hear yes or no without an explanation.

Those with a 1–3 in Fact Finder often make excellent marketing writers because they have the drive to communicate information succinctly, making the message understandable to someone who doesn't know anything about the subject.

4–6 in Fact Finder

Those whose strength lies in the mid-range of the continuum Accommodate the more extreme takes on gathering and sharing information seen at either end of the spectrum. They will naturally highlight what's important and bridge the gap between those taking the initiative and those pushing back. People with these mid-range strengths are vital to your team because they will extract the most essential facts and bring them to the team so everyone feels like they have the information they need to move forward.

How Do You Organize and Design?

Your strength in Follow Thru identifies how you organize and design. We've all met people who appear to be less organized or are self-proclaimed non-organizers. But whether it looks like it or not, everyone organizes in some way.

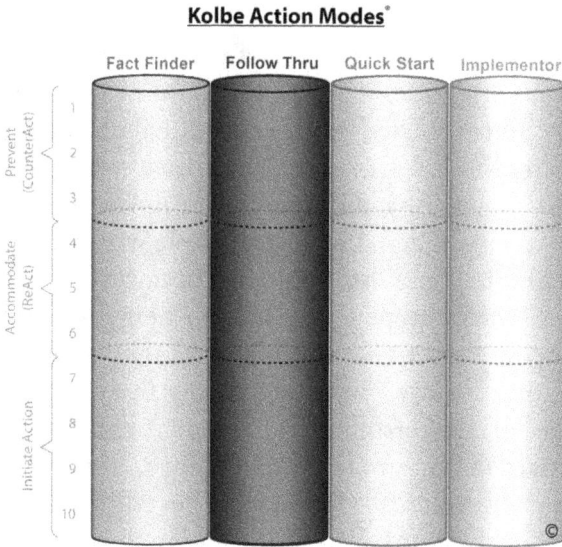

Kolbe Action Modes

7–10 in Follow Thru

A 7–10 in Follow Thru needs systems and plans. They Initiate by creating lists. Crossing off completed items gives them great satisfaction. Historically, the world has given the Initiating Follow Thrus permission to define what being organized looks like for everyone. Perhaps this is because even if we don't naturally work in this 7–10 zone of Follow Thru, we've all experienced the benefits that a structured approach provides.

We need the actions from the 7–10 end of the continuum to keep everything tidy and bring closure to projects. You'll often find pilots and teachers in this zone. They will naturally ensure that every step on the checklist gets checked off and revert to procedure when things aren't going according to plan.

1–3 in Follow Thru

On the opposite end of the Follow Thru continuum (1–3), we find those who look at the plan and immediately take shortcuts. These folks organize too, but their organization looks less traditional. Too many times, they've been told their method of organizing in piles isn't valid, and they're criticized for being disorganized. However, people with this strength shine when plans run into problems because they naturally skip unnecessary steps and adapt to new circumstances. These people Prevent bureaucracy, and they nicely balance the Initiating Follow Thrus by keeping their systems from becoming too cumbersome. The Resistant Follow Thrus can do their part and move on to other things, letting the 7–10s take the project across the finish line. Many salespeople work well in this zone. When the client changes the game plan, they easily follow the lead and switch gears. We could probably use more of them at the DMV.

4–6 in Follow Thru

Those who fall in the midrange in Follow Thru (4–6) don't necessarily need to create the plan but will Accommodate the system that is in place. They're great at tweaking it to improve efficiency and keep things moving forward productively. They can find the discrepancies and see the places where shortcuts won't work.

How Do You Deal with Risk and Uncertainty?

The Quick Start mode addresses the way you deal with risk and uncertainty. How do you naturally handle change? Do you attack problems with an innovative approach, or do you look for what is working and use the familiar to keep balance in your home or workplace? Neither way is wrong, and when people from both ends of the Quick Start continuum work together, amazing things can happen.

Kolbe Action Modes®

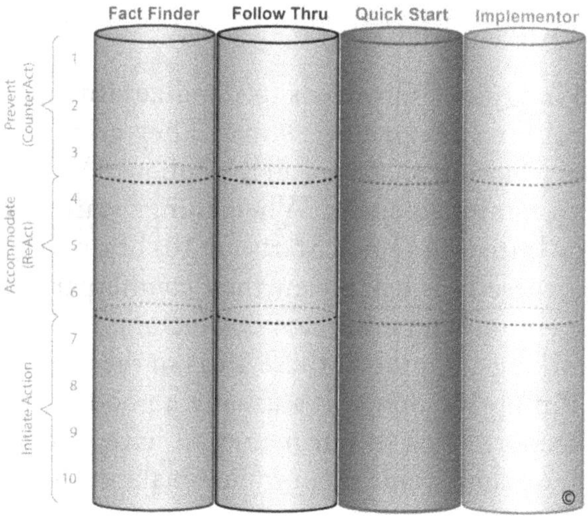

7–10 in Quick Start

The Initiating Quick Starts (7–10) do their best problem solving when they can experiment. They need to try out new things and create options. This group with the long green line is future-focused. They're constantly looking at alternative ways to approach a situation or take a risk to make things different. You can count on them to brainstorm and drive innovative solutions.

If you're working with an Initiating Quick Start, it's a good idea to give them short windows to work in. The pressure of deadlines engages them, and they often put things off if you give them too much time. You'll often find people with this strength are entrepreneurs or in outside sales. They naturally drive change to stay one step ahead of the marketplace.

1–3 in Quick Start

The 1–3 in Quick Start needs to stabilize situations when they encounter risk or uncertainty. They go into protect mode and will work to control all the options. We need them around to minimize chaos. When things start to change rapidly or Initiating Quick Starts (7–10) begin to push the envelope, these 1–3s will review their counterparts' ideas to filter the options and minimize risk factors. They see what is still working and protect those areas so the whole project doesn't flip upside down. It's usually a good idea for the people keeping track of our money to have this strength. After all, we don't want them to just make stuff up.

4–6 in Quick Start

The mid-range Quick Starts (4–6) adjust to change as needed. They probably won't drive the brainstorming sessions; however, they will sustain innovation initiated by others. They'll check out the new ideas before trying them and bring balance in uncertain times. We've seen people who fall in the 4–6 zone of Quick Start become great emergency room nurses. This group performs excellent triage even in the workplace.

How Do You Handle Space and Tangibles?

Everywhere you go, there are physical components, constraints, and objects to consider, and the Implementor mode tells the world how you best manage them.

Kolbe Action Modes

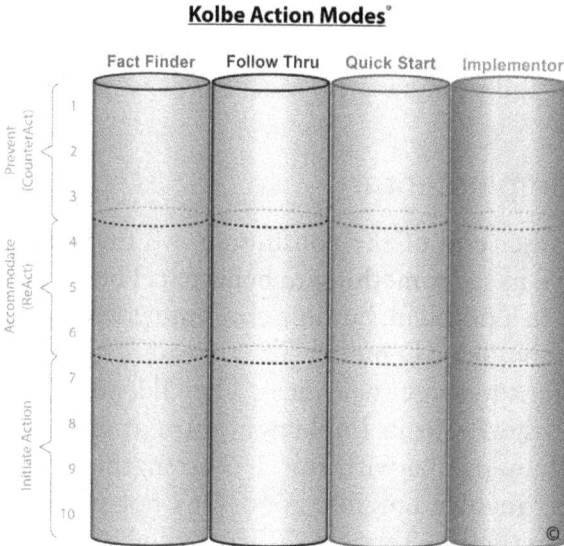

7–10 in Implementor

Initiating Implementors (7–10) are hands-on people. They take action in concrete rather than abstract ways. The longer the yellow line, the more you thrive when constructing and using tools or implements. These folks will most often fix things themselves or just build a new one from scratch. Those who fall in the 7–10 range on the Implementor continuum will show you how things work rather than tell you because they communicate best when they can physically demonstrate.

When it comes to technology, Initiating Implementors work on the hardware more than the software end of your devices. In the medical field, you'll find that many surgeons, chiropractors, and nurses have these longer yellow lines because they practice medicine by laying hands on people. Initiating Implementors use tools naturally, and they focus on physical quality. We find them in construction and manufacturing—any place where managing space, durability, building, and producing physical goods is needed.

1–3 in Implementor

At the other end of the continuum, we find people who don't have to see something to believe it. They imagine the solution to a problem, but in a conceptual way. They won't naturally build a 3D model. They create without needing to use props to share their ideas. They'll leave the physical work for the 7–10s in Implementor (or at least wish they had!). Many people with this 1–3 strength work in roles that don't involve tangible goods. It's not unusual for us to see them selling services rather than physical products. And although we talked about surgeons and nurses being in the 7–10 zone in Implementor, there is room for 1–3s in the medical field, too. General practitioners and those who work in internal medicine diagnose problems and prescribe care plans but don't need to be hands-on with tools and equipment the way a surgeon does.

4–6 in Implementor

Mid-range Implementors (4–6) tend to be pretty handy and contribute by repairing what's already there. They probably won't build something from scratch, but they keep things working well. They naturally make, restore, and remodel objects and machines and might have hobbies where they can work with their hands. Often, interior designers and others who bridge between the conceptual and physical have this strength.

Each of the 12 Kolbe Strengths is extremely valuable. A team with a diversity of these strengths represented has the potential to be stronger than one that doesn't and can be exponentially productive. Even if you don't have your Kolbe A, you will probably see yourself in some of these descriptions and recognize things you would do or not do if you were free to choose.

Some people don't have any of their strengths in the 7–10 zone. We call these people Facilitators. They easily switch between modes depending on what the situation needs, like someone with conative shape-shifting superpowers. Facilitators are invaluable in a team setting because they are great at holding everyone together and they naturally keep everything running smoothly. They're often the unsung hero, helping others behind the scenes work together more productively and fluently accommodating diverse needs.

There is another group we need to look at. About ten percent of the time, when someone answers the questions on the Kolbe Index, they aren't able to answer based on how they would take action if free to be themselves. When this happens, we don't know what their four Kolbe Strengths are yet. They receive a report with an asterisk instead of numbers on the chart. This means they received a Transition result. Everyone experiences Transition from time to time, especially during periods of great change like a new job or promotion, moving, caring for a sick family member, etc. Sometimes, individuals may attempt to answer in a way they feel someone else wants them to respond rather than answering the questions without any outside constraints. The good news is that once some time has passed and they are able to answer how they would if they were free to be themselves, they can retake the Kolbe A Index and find out their Kolbe Strengths.

Right or Wrong

For too long, people have been taught there is a right way and a wrong way to do things. Frustration builds on both sides when the person learning can't meet the expectations of the one doing the training—whether it's a parent, a teacher, or an instructor at work. You may not have embraced your natural strengths because the "right" way—the way other people have tried to make you operate—just doesn't work well for you.

Unfortunately, stereotypes also feed this problem. Women have been mistakenly labeled as the ones who keep things on schedule and are the best-organized planners. Men have stereotypically been thought of as the ones who should be handy and able to fix all the things that break. What we've seen is that there's not a conative difference by gender, age, or race. So, sure, some women are planners, but men are just as often, and while some men naturally work with their hands, so do women.

The problem is that sometimes, women who have a strength to be open-ended and find shortcuts around bureaucracy are told not to use those strengths because that's "not what women do." And sometimes, men hear they should be working with their hands, physically building and constructing things, even when that isn't how they naturally operate. In those cases, people are pigeonholed by these stereotypes and pushed into stressful, unproductive situations.

At Kolbe, we want to reshape mindsets and move from telling people how things should be done to painting a picture of excellence or the end result, giving everyone the freedom to be themselves while working toward their goals their way.

Just like your handedness is ingrained at birth, you have an innate way to get work done. Many of us have been trained to work in ways that don't align with our conative strengths. Everyone has the ability to work in all of the 12 Kolbe Strengths; after all, we're highly intelligent and capable of learning almost anything. But think back to those times when you've done what should have been a simple task, yet you felt completely drained when you were done. When we work against our natural conative strengths, we work slower, get frustrated, and expend more mental energy. It's a lot like writing your name with your non-dominant hand. Ultimately, we get poor results.

We spend a lot of time and money trying to better ourselves. And for the cognitive and affective parts of our mind, training could be a good investment. However, attempting to become "better" or change our conative strength in one of the Action Modes is just as ludicrous and foolish as concentrating our energy on changing our handedness.

We need to consider how often we're forcing ourselves to work against who we really are. And if we're part of a team, how often do we take our coworkers to this place of frustration?

Each time we say, "I need to be more . . .," we should think, "*Does that statement ring true for me, or do I need to find someone else to do this task?*" Alternatively, you might need to switch to working in one of your other conative strengths. As we've established, there are 12 Kolbe Strengths, but each person has four that are most natural for them. These four are your natural advantage—the secret to helping you Do More, More Naturally. Understanding your instinctive strengths will empower you to be yourself and give you permission to decide what deserves your best effort every day without putting in more hours. You will learn to say "no" when you're asked to constantly work outside your strengths in order to free up your precious mental energy for the things that matter most to you.

How Can My Kolbe Strengths Help Me?

Finding strengths in each of the Action Modes has been life-changing for millions. Some who felt as though life forced them to metaphorically write with their non-dominant hand found freedom in changing careers or redefining their job descriptions. Others learned how to work with the rest of their team more effectively, so they were less frustrated and more productive.

When you get your Kolbe result, it says, "Congratulations, you got a perfect score on the Kolbe A Index." We call your four Kolbe Strengths your MO, short for mode of operation or modus operandi. Too often, people think a higher number on the continuum is better; however, all four modes work together to create perfection. There is no good or bad, right or wrong. It's a revelation of how to most effectively tap into your mental energy to achieve the best results.

When we move into action according to our MOs, we enter that sweet spot because we're in the zone. We can go further and longer than ever before. However, when we aren't able to operate in our strengths zones, our mental energy will be depleted much more quickly, and we'll feel exhausted before the end of the day. Fortunately, like physical energy, mental energy is renewable through rest and relaxation.

The Kolbe Index can also help us understand those around us. As we begin to see their strengths and understand how they're different from ours, we can make our expectations more realistic and even laugh about our differences. When we apply this knowledge at home, we can adjust the way we treat our children. Rather than force them to complete tasks using the same methods we do, we can give them the freedom to reach the goal using their own unique conative strengths. We may need to give them guidance when they're young, but you'll be amazed at what even children can accomplish when allowed to problem-solve in their strengths zones.

Without clarity based on an understanding of the way they work conatively, employees with the greatest potential get transferred or hired for the wrong position, and they miss out on the joy of working in their zone.

Gaining clarity about your conative strengths is imperative. Knowing your capability for learning new things and understanding your personality is helpful as you interact with others and learn new skills. Nothing will increase your productivity, joy, and sense of success more than embracing your conative self and working in your strengths zones constantly and consistently. But getting there requires serious commitment.

Key Takeaways

1. Your four instinctive conative strengths come into play when you're striving and problem solving, not when you're at leisure.

2. Most problems and tasks can be accomplished in different ways. There is often not a "right" way or a "wrong" way to get things done.

3. Knowing your Kolbe Strengths can help you approach the things you care about in ways that come easier and are more natural for you.

PART TWO
Commitment

The difference between successful people and
really successful people is that really successful
people say "no" to almost everything.
—Warren Buffett

Chapter Five

What Is Your Superpower?

Gaining Clarity about your conative strengths is the first step, but how you commit to using those strengths determines the degree of stress you might have when getting things done. Commitment means making wise choices every single day regarding what is worthy of your finite mental energy. If we're truly serious about being able to Do More, More Naturally, we need to ask two simple questions: "What deserves my best efforts?" and "How can I avoid working against my grain?" Working against our innate capabilities causes burnout and frustration. Committing to our conative strengths empowers us to act in ways that add to our happiness and compel us to use our striving instincts to meet our highest potential. This commitment gives us permission to say "no" when someone suggests we take on a project outside our strength zones.

Committing to Being Yourself

Moving in your MO allows you to live with integrity. Your actions tell people, "I know who I am, what I need, and how I work best." Committing to your strengths clears the way to set healthy boundaries because you give yourself permission to say no based on who you are. You no longer feel bad when passing on the tasks that take you out of your game. Plus, knowing your strengths gives you the freedom to commit your mental energy to the places that matter to you. The disconnect between who you are and how you act has significant consequences. Feeling mentally drained is where it begins, but the resulting stress can lead to health problems and depression over time.

Commitment to your strengths allows you to be truly free to be yourself. Others who don't understand the conative part of the mind may attempt to suck you back into their definition of the right and wrong way to do things. Unless you commit to intentionally preserving your finite mental energy by staying in your zone, you'll find yourself struggling like an ant pushing a boulder up a hill. Our client John provides a good example.

John's cleaning business became extremely successful. He quickly secured a contract to clean private jets. Others envied his ability to start and grow a business in such a short time. But John couldn't enjoy his success. He kept hearing his dad's voice in his head. "You need a business plan. First, you need a long-term projection, then a process to meet short-term goals." While his friends congratulated him for everything he had achieved, John's dad scolded him for not doing his homework and downplayed the millions in revenue his son brought in each year. "You're just lucky," his dad told him. John's father believed there was only one way to run a successful business. He continually told his son to research the market, create a detailed business plan, and follow it to the letter.

When John received his Kolbe result, his eyes opened to his true potential and everything made more sense. He began to appreciate the way his dad tried to help him learn how to do business. Even without knowing his dad's specific conative strengths, John could tell the two of them were just wired differently. Understanding his Preventative (1–3) in Follow Thru strength gave him new insight. He told us he discovered that the way he started his company was the same way he continued to do business. "And I'm really good at it," he shared.

John's Clarity empowered him to embrace his best method of operation and validated his Commitment to working his way. It also turned off the voices in his head telling him he wasn't doing it right because he understood that his dad's action plan was right for his dad but not him. The only thing holding John back prior to his Kolbe Index was his own fear of what other people thought. He committed to saying "no" to the tasks that didn't fit who he was. Because he aligned his work with his strengths, he was able to maximize his mental energy and get more done in less time. Bonus, even though he put a tremendous amount of physical energy into his work, at the end of each day, he left energized.

John's actions are a great example of one of the 5 Rules for Trusting your Instincts: *Be Obstinate.*[7] He was able to stand his ground, even when he was being told that his approach was wrong by someone he loved and admired. Being obstinate doesn't mean you are uncooperative or difficult to work with. It does mean that you will have to learn to operate with grit and tenacity when the current environment or situation doesn't allow you to do things your way. This will help you develop resilience when you face obstacles and difficult decisions have to be made.

Perhaps you've lived with the philosophy "you can do anything you put your mind to." Many determined, smart people consistently get the job done. Unfortunately, they pay the price by reaching the limit of their finite mental energy. For these folks, knowing and committing to their conative strengths becomes extremely freeing.

Everyone is amazing at something. No one is amazing at everything (okay…maybe Wonder Woman comes close). Everyone has been endowed with the same amount of creative energy, but to take advantage of every bit, each person must learn to use their natural conative strengths and when to stop or say no. If you've ever flown, you've heard the spiel. "If something happens to the aircraft, oxygen masks will drop down. Please put your own on before you assist a child, the elderly, or someone who needs assistance." The airlines tell you this because they know you'll be worthless if you happen to pass out before you have an opportunity to help the person next to you. Just because you can doesn't mean you should. Those who perform at high levels have learned to be very strategic with their mental energy.

Committing to your innate strengths marks a turning point in life. That day becomes the start of giving yourself a break. Embracing your MO allows you to abandon the feelings of guilt when you don't want to do every task within your business just because you have the capability. It means you no longer say, "I should be better at this," and let go of the tasks that cause stress. Remember, all 12 Kolbe Strengths are critically important. Even though you can do all 12, the four that make up your MO are your superpower.

If you're tired of justifying your methods or explaining who you are, you'll find tremendous freedom in committing to your conative abilities. When you understand the way you're wired, you're better able to see how perfectly you were created.

Potential Roadblocks

Two primary things get in the way of using your mental energy efficiently. One is spending energy on low-level decisions or actions. When Mark Zuckerburg returned from paternity leave, he posted a picture of his closet with the caption, "What should I wear?" The social media picture showed a closet with nine matching gray t-shirts and seven gray hoodies. When asked about this, he said he has so many important decisions to make on any given day he refuses to spend one ounce of energy making frivolous decisions like choosing what to wear.[8] While we might not want to go to the Zuckerberg, Steve Jobs, or Homer Simpson uniform extreme, their clothing preferences demonstrate the unnecessary mental energy we spend on low-level decisions. Think about a day when you felt so depleted that by the time you got home, the simple decision about what to eat for dinner became overwhelming. This is decision fatigue. When we exert ourselves on unimportant tasks, we don't have any energy left for the things we truly care about—things that allow us to thrive.

Our second waste of mental energy lies in attempting to change ourselves. People spend a lifetime trying to do things in a way that's not natural for them, but it's just as productive as a plan to change your dominant hand. It's not a good use of your mental energy.

Whether you are right- or left-handed, as a child, you practiced writing to improve your skill. In the same way, we may decide we want to improve our scope of giftedness or the areas that bring us joy. Taking courses to learn new things and reading books to expand our knowledge can be valuable, but attempting to change our innate traits resembles a fish struggling to climb a tree.

Protecting Your Mental Energy

Unfortunately, as we said at the beginning, society has conditioned us to believe mentors, parents, or superiors do things better than we do. Even after we get clarity on our MO, it's difficult to shed those ideas handed down and ingrained in us.

Additionally, we've been taught that time management is the biggest issue we face, and the most important questions deal with our schedule: "Do I have time to do this task?" After all, much of what we have to do will take 10 minutes or less.

There are hundreds of paper and digital "solutions" to "managing" your time. And most only keep track of the things people blindly put on to-do lists. They focus heavily on the Do More side of the equation and disregard the More Naturally side, leaving most people's biggest issue unaddressed.

Being more successful is about doing more of the right things in a way that allows you the freedom to be yourself. We need to change the question. Rather than asking whether we have enough time, we need to ask, "Do I have the mental energy to do this?" or "Is this the best and highest use of my precious mental energy?"

Everyone has an equal amount of this instinct-driven mental energy, but it's finite. Even when you use your strengths in the most efficient way, you will run out. Our bodies and minds operate much like the vehicle in your driveway. If we go too far without stopping to refuel or recharge, we'll be stalled when we run out of energy. Abuse the vehicle too often, and you end up with a car that struggles to work at all. This does not mean you shouldn't commit fully to a given undertaking; it means you must make wise choices about what you commit to and what you don't. Kathy Kolbe said, *"Commit, but to very little and target your top priorities."*[9] It's necessary to assign different levels of effort to tasks that need to get done. Some things just need to get checked off the list, and others deserve your full energy. This shift in behavior is especially difficult if you grew up being told "anything worth doing is worth doing well" or have perfectionist tendencies. If you don't allocate your mental energy to the highest and best use of your strengths, you're wasting an important resource. The good news is that, unlike time, you can replenish it (more on this later).

By training our minds to understand our own ideal way to spend mental energy and committing our resources to stay within our MO, we can avoid the exhaustion the majority of the world experiences. Working outside our natural strengths is not only counterintuitive, but it can also be every bit as cumbersome, slow, and frustrating as writing with our non-dominant hands. This leads to stress that can be debilitating and result in physiological damage. We call this Conative Stress.

Mark O'Donnell, CEO of EOS Worldwide, who used to be an engineer in pharma, said this about his experience with Conative Stress: "When I worked in pharma, I had to deal with so much compliance; it took most of my time. I had to review 1,200-page documents and be able to point out the missing period on page 762. It was excruciating!

But I knew the medication was for babies in their first hour of life. And if I screwed it up, children would be at risk. So, I bottled up my strengths (2-2-10-3) and worked like I was 9 in Follow Thru instead of a 2 because I had to be. But at the end of the day, I just wanted to sleep for a year. I finally stopped doing it all myself and started a company of people who took care of those documents for the big pharma companies."

Mark O'Donnell
Kolbe A™ Result

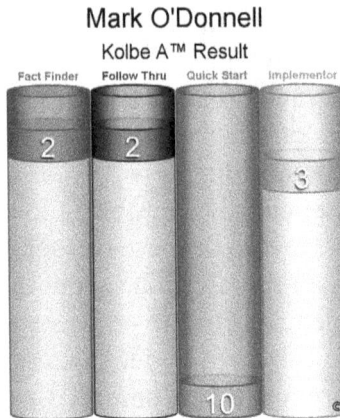

Fact Finder	Follow Thru	Quick Start	Implementor
2	2	10	3

We know it can be difficult to say "no" to people when you truly want to help them, but remember the analogy of the oxygen masks on the airplane. You're better able to give your best effort to colleagues when it doesn't cause yourself undue stress. We encourage you to prepare and practice scripts that you can use in these kinds of situations, like:

"I really need my energy to complete this task before moving on. Can we schedule a time later?"

"I'm not sure I have the right strengths for that. Have you considered asking _____ first? I'm happy to jump in once you need my Quick Start energy."

Perhaps we'd do better if we looked at our conative strengths as our superpower. Committing to your innate traits and giving yourself permission to be the person you were created to be brings more freedom than you ever imagined. When you work in your sweet spot—the place where your personality, intelligence, and natural strengths meet—you unleash a force as unstoppable as any Marvel or DC superhero.

Strive to Survive or Strive to Thrive

Striving sounds difficult, but if we live and breathe, we strive—it's part of life. And each bit of striving requires conative mental energy. Parenting, managing a household, and solving problems at work all demand some of our brain power. After we understand our instinctive strengths, we have the ability to direct our striving energy. We can choose to make all the hard work worthwhile. When we constantly work against our innate abilities, we live in survival mode. Some do it their entire lives, and they end up tired and miserable. Mark realized this before it was too late.

At Kolbe, we want your striving to result in thriving. We don't promise life will be easy, but sometimes it can feel effortless, even empowering. To get there, we need to stop trying to change ourselves. After all, Batman would never attempt to leap over buildings with a single bound. And we need to stop hiding our strengths, too. If you're Superman, don't be afraid to don the cape and save the day.

We are most effective when we embrace our natural strengths and commit to using the best of our mental energy to engage our superpowers.

Key Takeaways

1. Your mental energy is a finite resource you should guard and manage as much or more than your time.
2. There are frequently two ways you waste your mental energy: spending it on low-level problems or decisions and attempting to change yourself.
3. When you commit to operating according to your MO (natural strengths), you will be more productive and experience less stress.

Chapter Six
Good Advice Gone Bad

Perhaps you've read books or heard life coaches tell you everyone should create a to-do list and mark things off to be more productive. This works great for Initiating Follow Thrus (7–10), but if you're like John, you can call that tidbit "Good Advice Gone Bad." Not every method of organizing works for everyone.

We all know that exercise is important. In fact, surveys show that the vast majority of New Year's resolutions are fitness-related.[10] There are countless approaches that promise great results, but as it is with organizational methods, everyone has unique needs. An Initiating Quick Start will become bored without enough variety and challenge in their workouts, while those on the other end of the continuum thrive with a predictable program.

Unfortunately, we're surrounded by "Good Advice Gone Bad." We've all been inundated with well-meaning guidance and advice from parents, teachers, friends, and gurus for as long as we can remember, but there's no such thing as one-size-fits-all advice. Let's take a look at some familiar pieces of advice and the strengths they hinder.

Good and Bad Advice for the 7–10 in Fact Finder

Initiating Fact Finders thrive when they start with research. They need ample time to gather the facts and establish priorities. People with this strength need historical evidence and analogies, and sometimes their strategies may seem complex. If you have this strength, thriving means you'll commit to establishing specific priorities and assessing probabilities.

If you're working with a 7–10 in Fact Finder, and you want to help them succeed, give them as much information as you can or tell them where to find it. These folks need details. Additionally, you'll see them correct errors and ask questions until they thoroughly understand the specifics. Initiating Fact Finders won't be happy with generalizations or snap judgments, and if you're working with them, be prepared to go past yes or no with your answers.

Patricia is an Initiating Fact Finder. Pouring over details and double-checking stats allows her to contribute significantly to every project. When her coworker smiled and flippantly repeated the familiar phrase, "Don't sweat the small stuff, and it's all small stuff," he might as well have told her to stop breathing (more advice that we don't recommend). While that's sound advice for some folks, it's not for a 7–10 in Fact Finder. Patricia feels extra stress when she can't provide the information necessary to keep the project within specs.

If you do your best problem solving in this way, you shouldn't feel bad when you aren't prepared to give a spontaneous answer or make a decision without prioritizing your options. You were created to examine all the facts, and you need to get your responses right. Don't apologize for that.

Good and Bad Advice for the 7–10 in Follow Thru

Initiating Follow Thrus design tremendous sequential systems. Coordinating and integrating activities comes naturally to them. If you have this strength, everyone will come to you for exceptional planning, and their apparent disorganization might drive you a little crazy. Those who work with 7–10s in Follow Thru will want to make sure they close the loop on projects for them. They need to see things through to the end, even if it's just segments of a larger project.

Lisa finds joy in creating step-by-step plans that move the assignment across the finish line. When she discovers a hiccup in the process, and her boss tells her, "We'll cross that bridge when we come to it," his response simply sends her searching for the most productive way to cross that bridge and map out a few alternate paths to get there. She needs to have plans in place with backup plans before she is comfortable moving forward.

If you work with someone like Lisa, you might find they have a hard time with shortcuts. People who Initiate in Follow Thru will maximize their mental energy when they avoid interruptions and create checklists and schedules before the project begins.

Good and Bad Advice for the 7–10 in Quick Start

Initiating Quick Starts thrive on challenges and need to experiment. If you're a 7–10 in Quick Start, you'll be pushing the team forward on projects. Your race-the-clock and last-minute nature might drive others crazy (especially those with a 1–3 in Quick Start), but committing means you embrace your non-conformist nature.

Joe often uses his Initiating Quick Start instincts to concoct possible solutions. He improvises naturally and thrives on quickly trying out his ideas. Just because a project runs smoothly doesn't mean he won't have an idea to make it better. The worst advice you can give Joe is, "If it ain't broke, don't fix it."

Those who work with these brainstormers need to know Initiating Quick Starts shouldn't be expected to stick to the script. They thrive on newness, risk, and experimentation. And if this describes you, let your innate strength drive you. Don't hesitate or be afraid to fail. Your innovative forward-thinking will prove invaluable, so don't second guess yourself.

Good and Bad Advice for the 7–10 in Implementor

Initiating Implementors are in the zone when they get to work on tangible projects that require a hands-on approach. If you have this strength, you shouldn't be afraid to take your time and focus on quality. To make the best use of your mental energy, make sure you have the right tools for the job, and don't let anyone set unrealistic deadlines that force you to throw things together.

Maggie is an Initiating Implementor. You'll often find her creating prototypes, models, and displays. She naturally uses a "hands-on" approach to solve problems and will be happy to move things around in a three-dimensional mock-up to demonstrate her ideas. But when someone says, "Look, but don't touch," or "Can you just send me an email with the specs," she flounders.

If you work with someone like Maggie, expect them to require only the best tools and materials and to give you a show-and-tell as they demonstrate. Be sure to give this person plenty of time to complete their work because they are committed to providing tangible solutions that will last.

Good and Bad Advice for the Facilitators

Facilitators—those with no strengths in the 7–10 range—will thrive when they collaborate to solve problems. Since they Accommodate various methods of problem-solving, being part of a project team is an ideal use of their way of executing.

If you fall in the Facilitator category, it's important to avoid situations where you'll be required to spend the bulk of your day as an independent contributor. When you work on your own, you will be most productive with tasks or projects where at least some of the outcomes and processes are in place.

Steve is a Facilitator who naturally bridges the gap between the diverse needs of his teammates. Once someone Initiates activity, he instinctively facilitates the next steps to move the project forward. Often the unsung hero, he makes the team shine without taking the credit himself. The worst advice you can give him is to leave his team and strike out on his own.

If you work with a natural Facilitator, you need to understand that they shine when they help others succeed. They will flounder if you force them to work in a silo to get something done.

No Strength Is Unimportant

At the other end of each continuum, you'll find an instinctive strength just as vital as an Initiating one. And while these preventative strengths aren't where we begin to problem solve, we have to be just as committed to using them when our counterparts get a little carried away.

Those who have strengths in the 1–3 zones in each of the Action Modes use their strength to Prevent problems and Resist letting things go too far in that area.

Good and Bad Advice for the 1–3 in Fact Finder

The Preventative Fact Finder will sidestep the pesky details. They'll summarize, abbreviate, and get right to the point. If you need rough estimates or ballpark figures to complete your proposal, ask a 1–3 in Fact Finder rather than a 7–10.

Bill is a 1–3 in Fact Finder. His ability to simplify information is almost uncanny. The quickest way to kill Bill's creativity is to ask him to make a detailed list of priorities and justify his decisions. When his coworkers ask him to conduct a thorough analysis of the key variables, his stress level begins to rise immediately, and his productivity drops accordingly.

Preventative Fact Finders will give you metaphors and focus on the big picture. If you have this strength, don't get bogged down in the details or feel guilty if you can't justify your reasoning. Feel free to skim documents to pull out the most pertinent information and Resist reading the fine print.

Good and Bad Advice for the 1–3 in Follow Thru

Exhaustion sets in quickly when 1–3s in Follow Thru have to create or follow processes and procedures. Instead, they'll find shortcuts and thrive when they're working on multiple projects simultaneously. They need to keep everything they use often well within reach and won't mind trying random approaches to the project.

Mary used to feel guilty when she heard people tell her, "You should always finish what you start." It seemed like prudent advice. However, she gets bored when she works on the same project for very long or has to follow checklists and fill out forms. You can stop by her office and interrupt her anytime. She actually likes it, especially if you have a new problem to solve.

If you're working with someone like Mary, expect them to revise their approach and have a lot of irons in the fire. 1–3s in Follow Thru commit to being flexible and help you cut through the red tape. Additionally, they'll balance the most dedicated Initiating Follow Thrus because they will loosen up rigid processes.

Good and Bad Advice for the 1-3 in Quick Start

Preventative Quick Starts do things by the book. These folks will create standards for your organization and protect the status quo. If something's working, they will Resist changing it. They are completely committed to minimizing risk.

Michael is a 1–3 in Quick Start. Making changes causes him anxiety. So, when someone comes to him with a problem that needs to be addressed quickly, he's very uncomfortable. He might even freeze up if you tell him, "Try it; you'll like it." On the other hand, when things start to fly out of control, Michael will help you reduce the number of unexpected events and establish boundaries to protect the parts that still work properly.

Good and Bad Advice for the 1-3 in Implementor

People who are Preventative Implementors have the natural ability to imagine and conceptualize. They see things that don't exist yet and thrive in the abstract. They instinctively Resist it when someone tells them, "Roll up your sleeves" or "Get in there and get your hands dirty." That kind of hands-on approach causes pressure that takes them out of their strengths zone.

Sarah is a 1–3 in Implementor and envisions solutions but does not necessarily bring them into tangible reality. She'll give a general sketch of what she sees in her head, but don't ask her to construct a three-dimensional model. Ask Sarah and those like her to create your virtual presentations and capture the essence of your ideas. If you need someone to conceptualize your solution, these Preventative Implementors will be your best allies.

Take a Lesson from Goldilocks

Our natural instincts help us flourish in problem solving, and if you haven't experienced what it's like to work in the zone, you're missing out on tremendous opportunities to thrive. There's also a good chance you've been underusing, overusing, or misusing your natural abilities.

Underusing your strengths can cause frustration because deep down, you know you have a great deal to offer; however, the tasks you have to do cause you to feel empty because they don't capitalize on your conative strengths. Other times, you withhold the contributions your strengths would make because the purpose or values of a particular effort or organization don't align with yours. Either way, the work isn't fulfilling for you.

Getting stuck in inaction is another way that you could be underusing your strengths. You might experience challenges like this for some of the reasons mentioned earlier, like overthinking decisions or waiting around to feel motivated.

It's at times like these that you'll need to kick yourself into gear and follow Kathy's advice to Self-Provoke.[11] No one can do it for you.

Some of the critical things that need to be done are not going to be fun or pleasant, but they are necessary for you to achieve your goals. As author Mel Robbins says bluntly, "You are never going to feel like it." There is a myth that successful people are motivated to do the tough stuff, but that's simply not true. They know it's all about momentum. Using your strengths to get a few small wins leads to the increased motivation needed to keep going. We've all experienced how momentum is helpful when developing a new habit, like exercising regularly. The same concept applies to using your strengths. Ultimately, if you're working in alignment with your strengths most of the time, you won't need *to Self-Provoke* as often.

Overuse can be just as easy a trap to fall into as underuse. The excitement of understanding their strengths causes some bright, talented individuals to forget how to say no or rein it in when it's time to stop. Worthy projects present themselves, and those energetic souls jump on them. While you have more mental energy when working with your striving strengths, it's still finite. Whether you're at work, at home, or in a volunteer position, overusing your strengths isn't any more beneficial than underusing them.

Misuse comes into play when we begin to impose our natural strengths on others or use them to dodge responsibilities. Some even capitalize on their strengths in order to manipulate or cause harm to others. Imposing our strengths on others isn't always deliberate or malicious. It often happens when we aren't even aware of our own bias toward a specific method of problem-solving. If a sales leader learned to sell by following a script, they may demand that their team do the same. They could inadvertently be adding tremendous stress to those who sell most effectively when they can improvise. Another example of misuse is to use your strengths as a copout to avoid doing something critically important. The IRS isn't going to accept tax computations that are "close enough" with your excuse that you don't naturally handle the details.

The key to minimizing underuse, overuse, and misuse of your strengths is to become increasingly aware of which situations might cause these and continue on the journey to find the highest and best use of your unique talents. Much like Goldilocks when she found the porridge and the bed that was just right, when we give ourselves permission to commit our mental energy wisely, we'll find ourselves happier and energized to live life to the fullest.

The Myth of 10,000 Hours

Forty years ago, Herbert Simon and William Chase shared an observation now known as the 10,000-hour rule. In an article in *American Scientist*, they said, "There are no instant experts in chess—certainly no instant masters or grandmasters. There appears not to be on record any case (including Bobby Fischer) where a person reached grandmaster level with less than about a decade's intense preoccupation with the game. We would estimate, very roughly, that a master has spent perhaps 10,000 to 50,000 hours staring at chess positions..." Malcolm Gladwell added that innate talent was also required, and still, the gifted need 10 years of preparation to reach the highest level of ability.[12]

This 10,000-Hour Rule perpetuates one of life's greatest myths—if you possess enough determination, you will reach your fullest potential. When combined with an attitude that we should never back down from a challenge, the myth produces people who spend thousands of hours moving from good to pretty good. Too many experts try to convince us that our weaknesses are challenges to be taken on as if it's more noble to accept the challenge of a weakness than it is to achieve our goals using our strengths. Of course, there are times when you may have to develop cognitive skills or affective abilities if they are negatively affecting your work or personal life. But our natural instincts are already perfect for us.

Kolbe Corp challenges people to focus on their instinctive strengths. We want people to have the freedom and Clarity to Commit their energy to achieve goals that tap into their cognitive, affective, and conative strengths.

Occasionally, we'll get some pushback from people who think we're telling them not to do anything difficult. That couldn't be further from the truth! Some folks live for the challenge. They love to try new things, learn to play an instrument, conquer mountains, or change the world. Our passion is to help people achieve their goals, whether they seem simple or monumental. We love high expectations and audacious goals. What we hate is seeing people handicap themselves, making it harder to achieve what they set out to do.

Perhaps you want to win a gold medal in swimming. Before you begin, it's important to know if your body is better equipped for swimming long or short distances. If you have world-class explosiveness at the beginning of a race but lack the stamina to maintain that fast pace lap after lap, you should be a sprinter, not an endurance swimmer. The goal to win a gold medal remains, and it will still take a lot of work. But knowing your strengths and capitalizing on them makes the goal more achievable.

The same is true with our mental strengths. Yes, we can learn to do nearly anything cognitively, but how much of our finite mental energy supply do we want to spend trying to become a master of something that will never be natural to us? Someone who has an inborn talent for music might find it worthwhile to commit the time and energy to learn a new instrument. However, if you struggle to learn the basics, is devoting hours to the craft a good investment of your resources? Why would you spend your limited time and energy raising your level of competence to mediocre when you could invest the same resources to become excellent in an area you're already passionate about? Dan Sullivan of Strategic Coach, whose story we shared at the beginning, once said, "If you work throughout your life on improving your weaknesses, what you get are a lot of really strong weaknesses."

Consider Fred—a master carpenter whose business grew to the point he found himself relegated to sales and invoicing. It's not that he couldn't take care of administrative work. It's just that his 7–10 in Implementor felt stifled doing paperwork. He found his mental energy drained quickly when forced to describe the work to clients rather than build the finished product and develop new skills in his craft.

At Kolbe, we encourage you to push yourself into fresh and exciting things. However, years of research prove when you do it within your MO, the difficult feels effortless.

Strengthening the Conative Muscle

We don't want to discourage anyone who wants to get an Olympic medal; we simply think you should be smart about it. If you love to run but you're not a strong runner, you won't choose the Boston Marathon for your first major event. You start by jogging a mile before you try a 5K; then you move on to a 10K, and eventually, you can accomplish your dreams.

The same is true of your conative strengths. If you constantly lived with your strengths being pushed to the bottom or dismissed, you may need some practice developing them. Suppose you're in the 7–10 range on Follow Thru—the thought of systems and organization excites you. At the same time, if you were raised in a household full of people in the 1–3 or 4–6 ranges, you may have never had the opportunity to put systems or organization in place. In the beginning, working in your zone might feel awkward or even uncomfortable. Because of your formative environment, the first time you try to create a system, success may only last two minutes. You must choose: Will I give up, or will I push to work in my zone and learn everything I can about this strength until I excel?

Anyone who lifts weights will tell you building muscles can be painful. The discomfort can last days or weeks. But they'll also tell you that when you work muscles the wrong way, the pain is worse, and when you're doing it right, you get better results and a faster recovery. Perhaps you've known dancers, musicians, or artists who weren't encouraged to live out their natural talents until later in life. Even with no lessons or studies in technique, when they finally begin to pursue those talents and dedicate time to perfecting them, they pick them up quicker than most. Thankfully, the same will happen when you embrace your conative strengths and learn to develop them. Even while it's uncomfortable, the tasks we accomplish using our MO will feel natural, and the skill will develop instinctively and more quickly than if we were attempting to build muscles outside the strengths we were born with.

Let's go back to the handwriting exercise. It doesn't make sense to spend time and energy strengthening our non-dominant hands. However, many have spent valuable hours strengthening their dominant hands while they practice holding the appropriate tool to write in calligraphy, create wood carvings, or become a master mechanic. It's not a matter of what you should or should not learn to do or even how challenging the new endeavor is. The wise choice will always be dependent on how much mental energy you should expend to master the craft.

Key Takeaways

1. There's no such thing as one-size-fits-all advice.

2. All of your Kolbe Strengths are important to consider, especially when deciding which advice to listen to and which to dismiss.

3. Many people have spent their entire lives doing things in ways that aren't natural for them. Changing that behavior might feel awkward at first, but it will become much easier than what wasn't natural.

Chapter Seven

It's Time to Stop Swimming Against the Current

Swim spas, or endless pools, have become a popular exercise tool. These oversized hot tubs provide a constant current so you can practice your breaststroke in place. But while they provide excellent cardio, the swimmer never moves forward. That's what it's like when we choose to work outside our MO. We work hard, get tired from swimming against the current, and go nowhere.

In an ideal world, we would easily find roles aligned with our conative strengths and get to do those jobs in a way that was natural for us almost all the time. Unfortunately, void of those idyllic conditions, we must be intentional about working with our innate abilities. When we refuse to spend the majority of our time and energy swimming against the current and instead commit to our strengths, we discover the ability to stay in the zone and can Do More, More Naturally.

Staying in the Zone

We've all been assigned tasks that bored us and stole every ounce of joy. And even after you begin to understand yourself, occasionally, you'll still need to perform some of those mundane tasks. However, the feeling of tremendous frustration and burnout only appears when we consistently work against our grain. When we're allowed to take action instinctively, we accomplish more in less time and have fun doing it. We get lost in our work, and our production ramps up.

Steven Kotler calls the feeling "flow"—a state of being in the moment, not worried about whether to turn right or left. The answers appear naturally. Psychologists Mihaly Csikszentmihalyi and Jeanne Nakamura popularized the idea. Csikszentmihalyi described it as a state of "focus that, once it becomes intense, leads to a sense of ecstasy, a sense of Clarity: you know exactly what you want to do from one moment to the other."[13] That's what happens when we commit to staying in our strengths zones as often and as long as possible.

It's like a professional baseball player standing at the plate. He's not thinking about the pitch. He's just watching the ball, doing what comes instinctively. When those players are left to use their innate strengths, they get in the zone. The ball looks fat. It seems to move in slow motion, and they can hit it out of the park. After all, one of the most popular baseball films of all time is literally called *The Natural*.

Amy's Story

Amy's husband, Jim, was a professional pitcher whose coach took action in the exact opposite way he did. When he hit a slump, his coach kept trying to advise him, but it wasn't working. His coach offered detailed explanations on how to improve his form; however, Jim is an Initiating Implementor (7–10) and learns best with a physical demonstration.

Kathy heard about his struggle and offered some wisdom based on the way he best takes action. First, she told him to listen to his coach and nod and smile. Obviously, his coach knew a lot about pitching and deserved Jim's respect. Kathy went on to tell him that after he listened to the coach's advice, he needed to watch the film and pay attention to the way his body felt. He would best correct his pitching mechanics by leveraging his natural strengths and physically feeling his body work versus listening to details regarding how it should work. The results were amazing. By leveraging his innate strengths, he turned his season around.

This state of flow and the ability to make great strides in your career aren't limited to baseball players. One of the goals at Kolbe Corp is to reshape the mindset around the way people accomplish tasks. The world spends a lot of time, energy, and money retraining the brightest and best to complete tasks in cookie-cutter ways rather than allowing them to shine by using their own strengths. Because these folks pick up new skills quickly, they adapt. However, it ultimately results in frustration.

How Do We Know When to Commit?

Understanding your four conative strengths gives you the power to know when to say "yes" or "no". You can't spend every moment in striving mode. You need some downtime to replenish your mental energy. When evaluating what you're going to do or not do, remember to ask yourself, "Do I have the mental energy to do this? What's the highest and best use of my strengths?"

Additionally, ask, "What one task causes me the most stress?" Every undertaking has three potential reasons to drain you. It could be cognitive. You might not have the knowledge required to complete the task, and more training will take care of the angst; at other times, you might need to enlist help. Your stress could also stem from your personality or preferences. Maybe the job just doesn't fit who you are—it needs an extrovert, and you're an obvious introvert. There's also the possibility the work doesn't align with your values or what you enjoy in a work environment.

But often when we feel as though a job is mentally draining, it's because a particular task doesn't fit our conative strengths. Commitment to operating at your best means finding others whose strengths are a better fit and giving yourself permission to bow out of parts of projects that fall outside your zone.

Of the hundred or so different tasks your work and home life require of you in any given month, it would not be unusual to say only five fall into the category of tasks you love. As you allow the knowledge of your innate strengths to bring Clarity to how you do things, you can do some simple exercises to show you when to Commit that mental energy.

Task Analysis Activity

1. One activity we complete with clients involves a close examination of the things they do down to the task level. Make a list of two or three of the most frustrating or draining things you do—even the simple and straightforward ones.

2. Look at your list one by one and consider how often each task takes you outside your MO.

3. Rate them according to how well the tasks fit your instinctive strengths:

   1 = Great fit, 2 = Ok fit, 3 = Not a fit.

4. Next, estimate what percentage of your time each day you spend working against your grain. What would decreasing this percentage by 10 percent of the time do for you?

Let It Go

After you've completed your list, consider which of these tasks could you let go of in order to work within your MO. If you can live without it, delete it. You may need to let go of perfection or stop feeling the need to justify yourself. Challenge your expectations of what is really necessary.

This list can include personal tasks as well as assignments at work. For instance, overextended parents should not feel guilty when they limit the number of activities their children can participate in or when they delegate tasks other parents relish. Not everyone needs to be the "Team Mom." Demonstrating the beauty of working within your strengths and spending quality time with your children, even when it's less traditional, gives them definite advantages later in life.

As you evaluate your list and make adjustments accordingly, you'll see how small changes can reap big rewards when you move closer to working in your zone for longer stretches of each day. Operating in your superpower doesn't mean you can or should do it all.

We encourage people to write down the things they want to let go of and run the paper through a shredder. "If it doesn't fit, you must shred it." The act of writing and seeing what you want to change in print increases your likelihood of success by about 42 percent.[14] Shredding that paper releases the old advice and guilt and symbolizes you granting yourself permission to let go and begin to swim with the current.

Give It Away

After you decide what you want to let go of, consider those tasks that leave you feeling amazing and accomplished. If you analyze the intelligence, personality, and conative strengths you use to carry out those few enjoyable tasks, you'll find your sweet spot. To get into that state of flow more often and for longer periods of time, we must figure out what to do with those frustrating tasks you cannot just delete. What could you take off your list by delegating? Maybe you think it's faster to do it yourself than to train or explain it to someone else. You'll have to remind yourself it's not about time management; it's about mental energy. We encourage you to ask yourself, "Who has the right strengths and skills to do this?" And then, give it a try. If you're not the leader of a team or you lack natural delegation partners, challenge yourself to think of outsourcing, automation, or using AI to help.

Do It More Naturally

As we let go of things that don't fit, we make room for the tasks that better use our mental energy. After these first moves, it's all about small changes. Once a month or more, commit to doing one more thing in a more natural way to get into the zone. Keep your eyes open for new technology solutions. New apps and programs that can both enhance your strengths and ease the burden of working against them hit the app stores every day.

Delegating or finding a partner to help with a stressful task you can't delete can go a long way. Most tasks can be broken into multiple parts. Shannon Waller of Strategic Coach says the one depleting task she must get help with is her calendar. Her assistant handles the logistics and then runs them by her for approval. This one shift frees up her mental energy for much more important pursuits.

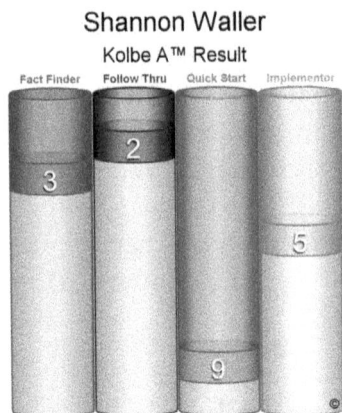

Shannon Waller
Kolbe A™ Result

My Kolbe MO is 3-2-9-5, and with my 2 in Follow Thru, my mental energy for scheduling gets depleted very quickly. [It's pretty much used up by the time I'm finished getting ready and to work on time.] When I finally decided to hire a full-time Executive Assistant, it freed me up enormously. Her MO is 6-7-3-3, and for her, scheduling is like playing a game of Tetris®. She takes great satisfaction in artfully arranging the calendar to maximize the opportunities while making sure I don't get overscheduled or burnt out. What she thrives on gives me stress! It has tripled my productivity—I can accomplish so much more when she is laying out the track in front of me and handling the follow-up from my appointments and projects. What I can do on my own is limited; what we can do together is exponential.

Everyone encounters times when they're forced to work against their natural strengths. Your main objective will be to limit your time there to short bursts. But if you're a solopreneur, you may be forced to do unpleasant tasks until you find an opportunity to hire someone with the strengths to take them off your plate. If that's the case, a little creativity might be just the trick to keep you sane.

Stephanie hated bookkeeping. She was quite capable, but the systematic nature of accounting tasks made it tedious for her 1–3 strength in Follow Thru. Until she could afford to add another person to her staff, she made the task as pleasant as possible by joining several other solopreneurs for "Beers and Bookkeeping." The group would gather at regular intervals to catch up on these repetitive tasks while sharing some camaraderie. Although she never thought drunk accounting was a good idea, it was a genius move to get her most stressful task completed. (Our lawyer is requiring us to add a disclaimer here that we in no way intend to encourage anyone to bookkeep while intoxicated!)

At times, people on the 1–3 end of the Fact Finder continuum will need to provide detailed plans, and Initiating Follow Thrus (7–10) will be forced to start a project before the plan has been solidified. You may never be as systematic, structured, and organized as someone whose natural instinct is to see things through to the end; still, your boss and co-workers won't tolerate you putting off jobs for weeks or months because your Preventative Follow Thru (1–3) strength instinctively moved on to the next task or project. Fortunately, embracing your superpower will help you understand why you're not comfortable with it. Just recognizing the source of the stress can alleviate the pain a bit. And your Commitment to your strengths will give you permission to limit the amount of mental energy you spend in that area.

Eric is one of the members of the Kolbe team. He thrives as a 9 in Quick Start with a 3 in Follow Thru. Growing up, his dad offered great-sounding advice: "Proper planning prevents poor performance." At first glance, this phrase makes perfect sense. However, Eric's dad is a 2 in Quick Start and an 8 in Follow Thru. His go-to method is systematizing and planning.

To follow his dad's advice, Eric used to try to work systematically; however, almost as soon as he started a project, his need for flexibility would kick in and scrap the plan while his Quick Start came up with lots of new approaches. After he learned more about how he operated, he stopped spending his mental energy creating a process and realized he just needed a jumping-off point. His strengths allowed him to adjust as needed.

Eric also realizes that managing a team means operating with a schedule and being a bit structured. Because he couldn't delegate or get help with his scheduling, he had to develop a strategy that would allow for the flexibility he needed, so he put a little hack in place. He gives everyone in the office access to his calendar, and they all have permission to put themselves on it anytime they need to meet with him. He depends on his scheduling program to notify him a few minutes before each meeting so he can be on time. And he decided not to operate from a different calendar for personal things—his wife adds items just like his staff does. It would drive Initiating Follow Thrus crazy not to know what their schedule looked like hours in advance, but he thrives on interruptions. This frees him to work in his strengths zone while meeting the needs of his team.

Working outside your natural strengths on a regular basis will cause burnout. And if your job continually forces you to work outside your MO, it might be time to find a new career. Therefore, it's vital to learn how to determine if adapting and working against your grain will add to the productivity of your team or make things easier at home.

You have to ask yourself if the value you bring to the project by working outside your strengths is worth exerting the extra energy and risking burnout.

Using our strengths appropriately allows those around us to reap the benefits as well. When we Do More, More Naturally, our increased productivity and joy ripple over onto our friends, family, and coworkers.

Key Takeaways

1. Consistently working against your grain puts you at greater risk for burnout.

2. Understanding your own instinctive strengths helps you make wise Commitments and gives you the power to know when to say yes or no.

3. Sometimes, the best thing to do with tasks that take you out of your zone is to let them go, partner with someone, or give them away altogether.

Chapter Eight

Recharging Your Battery

In this day of cell phones, laptops, and cordless everything, we understand the concept of recharging. Most don't realize the same principle applies to humans. We can only keep going for so long. Unfortunately, when humans continually push past their limits, something has to give. Burnout sets in or worse. Even the Energizer Bunny®'s battery runs down eventually. To use your innate strengths to their ultimate potential, you need to take time to recharge.

Permission to Procrastinate

Everyone has heard the phrase, "Stop procrastinating." Perhaps you've even scolded yourself for putting things off. While procrastination can be a detriment, it can also give you an opportunity to move forward in your strengths most effectively.

Procrastination most often has its roots in one or more of the three parts of the mind. If we aren't confident we have the knowledge or skill to complete the task, we probably won't even want to start. The affective part of our mind will stall us if we don't want to do the assignment or know we won't enjoy it. Boredom can also steal our motivation. On the other hand, putting things off can also be a signal that those tasks are outside your MO or require more mental energy than you have at the time, or perhaps that you are overcommitted, have too much on your plate, or need to recharge. Pay attention to when you procrastinate. It may be a sign for you to delegate, delete, or recharge.

For example, an Initiating Fact Finder will get stalled when the project they've been asked to lead is missing critical data. At the other end of the continuum, if Preventative Fact Finders find themselves buried in details, they will drag their feet because they won't know where to start.

On the Follow Thru spectrum, the 7–10s will lag without a plan in place to reach the finish line. At the same time, the 1–3s find themselves stuck when forced to follow a rigid process.

Since urgency and risk drive Initiating Quick Starts, procrastination hits them when the project lacks a pressing deadline or the ability to experiment. On the other hand, the Preventative Quick Starts will put the project off if there are too many options or it seems risky.

Initiating Implementors who seem to be dawdling probably feel forced to deal in abstract concepts or haven't been given the appropriate quality materials. However, if any hands-on building or fixing is necessary, those who fall on the 1–3 end of the continuum will drag their feet as long as possible.

Finally, Facilitators will procrastinate when they have no one or nothing to respond to. Being forced to work independently will surely reduce momentum for them.

When you find yourself in one of those situations, give yourself permission to procrastinate just long enough to find a different approach. Let managers and leaders know what causes the hesitation or find someone whose MO is a better fit for the activity and delegate. We need to stop beating ourselves up when we leave something until the last minute or ask someone else to accomplish tasks that don't merit our best efforts. Most people spend their lifetimes feeling guilty because they procrastinate or avoid tasks. However, when we commit to Do More, More Naturally, we can use procrastination as a tool to identify tasks that will require too big a chunk of our mental energy and aren't worthy of it. And, if you let it, procrastination will give you permission to say "no."

Give Yourself a Break

You deserve to figure out exactly how to find the freedom to be yourself—to have true joy in your everyday work and build more rewarding relationships. We can't state it enough: Everyone has a finite amount of striving mental energy. Once you've run out, it needs to be replenished. You get diminishing returns when you continue to work longer hours when your mental energy is depleted. Eventually, you'll see your productivity drop to 80 percent, then 50, and at some point, you may even be doing damage.

If you've ever driven a vehicle after the oil light comes on or ignored the mechanic's advice about how often to change your oil, filters, and lubricants, you've probably encountered the engine damage that occurs without proper maintenance. Just like your car needs more than gas to keep it running well, you need regular rest, nutrition, and care to keep producing at your highest level.

This Commitment to preserving your mental energy goes beyond the workplace. Your personal life requires problem solving and decision making as well. Your family and friends deserve the best of you. Don't forget the rule about oxygen masks on planes. You cannot effectively help others and take care of the most important people in your life if you don't take care of yourself first.

Vacations can be a chance to relax and recharge. But what should be a fun trip can end up being more draining than rejuvenating. How many times have you heard someone say, "I need a vacation to recover from my vacation?" This might stem from long flights, time differences, or trying to cram so much into a short time period. But conative differences can also cause problems and stress. Fortunately, if you understand them, they can be used to your advantage.

David's Story

I naturally embark on open-ended adventures, creating opportunities for spontaneous experiences. My wife Pam plans trips with excursions and outings woven into our schedule. I appreciate the way her planning makes things run smoothly, as well as the time she spends on the trip's logistics. This talent that comes so naturally to her would be torture for me. The truth of the matter is I find it annoying and stressful when the whole vacation is planned in advance. (Even creating slots for enforced "downtime" doesn't fit my MO.) When there's no time to explore or take advantage of last-minute opportunities, I feel frustrated. On the other hand, Pam gets frustrated when "last minute opportunities" turn chaotic, especially if that messes up other plans.

So yes, we've both been "unfairly" annoyed with each other when parts of a trip weren't going our way. The solution is for both of us to get to use our strengths. I research things ahead of time, and she makes plans that include blocks of time for me to explore, then I take the lead to get us moving.

The Freedom to Do Nothing

Sometimes you need to stop striving and do nothing. We need to give ourselves permission to take some time to replenish this precious resource. It's vital to discover your unique way of recharging.

Some find their energy replenished when they take in nature or enjoy music. As these peaceful moments touch their senses, they can feel themselves recharging. Others end their day with a good workout or a dance class. Even though their physical bodies feel tired when they are done, their mental energy tanks refill.

Crafts, gardening, and other hobbies that don't require heavy problem solving fulfill many individuals' requirements for a mental energy boost. And if you're the person who needs something more passive that allows you to completely turn off your brain, you shouldn't feel guilty. You might feel extremely energized after watching television or napping.

Logging on to social media or gaming might seem like a good way to chill, but it's important to consider how you feel after. Scrolling on social may seem like a good break, but not if it causes you to feel more frustrated or depleted.

If you've ever met Kathy Kolbe or watched one of her video interviews, you may have heard her boast that her ability to get so much done even at her age is because she knows how to do nothing. One of the rules she lives by is to *Do Nothing When Nothing Works*.[15] She understands the necessity for moments of peace and quiet. Too many times, we feel as if a lack of activity means we're lazy; however, committing your mental energy to your MO and recognizing the finite nature of your mental energy gives you permission to relax, take walks, read, and enjoy your friends and family.

In one interview, Kathy said she doesn't cook because "Why would you spend your life doing things you don't like doing?" Though she's stepped back from Kolbe Corp, and she makes restoring her mental energy a priority, she's still tremendously productive—not because she does more or manages time better. She experiences high performance because she owns her limited mental energy and uses it wisely.

Allowing yourself to recharge through strategic procrastination and doing nothing is critical for committing to your strengths effectively and sustaining high performance. But Clarity and Commitment are only the beginning. Gaining clarity and truly committing to your strengths reveals the importance of the third part of the Three C's. Those who live in the beauty of their strengths soon discover they can't do it alone. Collaboration becomes the essential piece that multiplies your results. It's this third C that propels us to success and makes striving more fun.

Key Takeaways

1. Mental energy is finite. Recharging your mental energy needs to be a priority for everyone to achieve peak performance.

2. The things you procrastinate most can be a clue into the things that take you out of your zone.

3. Ask yourself, "What is my most effective way to stop striving and do nothing?"

PART THREE
Collaboration

Talent wins games,
but teamwork wins championships.
—Michael Jordan

Chapter Nine

Making Beautiful Music

Now that you know how to focus on your strengths and commit your mental energy to working in your zone, it's time to take your strengths into the real world. Life requires interaction and connection with others. Sure, this can mean frustration and compromise, but it also means support, Collaboration, and greater accomplishments.

Entrepreneurs often start as solopreneurs, and many feel better working alone—they just don't want to deal with people. Unfortunately, if you aren't willing to ask for help in your business, you put a cap on your success because you limit the amount of work you can accomplish in 24 hours and risk burning out. To achieve big goals and reap the corresponding rewards, you almost always have to collaborate with others who have skills and problem-solving approaches that complement your own.

When groups of people have the help and support of others who bring new skills, approaches, and energy, they can accomplish things impossible for the same number of people working as individuals. Because of our finite mental energy and unique natural strengths, it's imperative we figure out who to surround ourselves with to make collaborations successful. Yes, things might get messy, but that's expected and manageable as long as you know what's happening with the group dynamics.

Should You Go Solo or Get a Team?

You are probably a part of multiple teams, including collaborations with your family and colleagues at work. Each team has a different mission, requiring different levels of interaction. When people work together, team dynamics can make or break results. Understanding your team makeup predicts where you might struggle.

If you're the strong, intelligent, independent type, there's a good chance you've learned to power through to get things done on your own. As a rugged individualist, you are amazing all by yourself. Many people who experience success have those kinds of capabilities.

Maybe one of the reasons you've decided to work in isolation is that when you've worked with others in the past, things didn't get done or didn't get done the way you would have done them. We're sure you know someone—maybe it's you—who won't let anyone else load the dishwasher or fold the towels because no one else does it right. In the business world, this might look like the entrepreneur who won't let his assistant manage his calendar or the person in charge of procurement who refuses to allow anyone else in her department to place an order without her approval. Those household folks waste precious time and energy reloading the glasses and plates and doing jobs someone else can do. However, in the business realm, this micromanagement equates to lost productivity and increased payroll expenses. When we cling to a method outside our strengths just because we think we have the only solution, it seems just as pointless.

Bringing a bunch of different personalities and conative strengths into the same room can produce the same kind of friction if you don't understand the dynamics. Some become frustrated, while others take the pushback personally. It's tempting to retreat and try to forge ahead on our own rather than work through the challenges of collaborating with those who do things differently.

Unfortunately, while this "do it myself" mindset can be more comfortable, it's usually not productive. When you consider the frustrations of working with others, the time it takes to smooth out the wrinkles, and the pain involved in figuring out how to add the right people, you might be thinking, "Why bother?"

According to the United States Small Business Administration, 80 percent of firms across the United States have no employees. These solopreneurs take care of everything themselves, and they average about $47,000 in revenue each year. However, by adding just four or fewer employees, those same businesses increase revenue by more than $340,000. Adding only a few people starts to give rugged individualists the freedom to focus on using their strengths, which allows even the average company to earn seven times more revenue.[16]

Musical collaborations work best when the players listen to and feed off each other's creativity. Sure, one person playing an instrument can perform a great solo, but most music that moves the soul comes from the collaboration of great artists. Elton John and Bernie Taupin combine their talents with music and lyrics. Orchestras blend multiple people playing multiple instruments to create cohesive symphonies. Even solo acts like Taylor Swift collaborate with producers, other singers, songwriters, and musicians to take their songs from raw ideas to the complete pieces of music we stream and listen to at concerts.

These collaborations aren't always, or even usually, easy. Sometimes, their musical styles don't mesh well, or their personalities clash, but when they work together, they can create magic. Reaching exponential performance levels doesn't mean simply adding warm bodies. The perfect teammates need the right attitude, intelligence, and instinctive strengths. It's way more fun and productive to work with people when they're a great fit in all three areas. We've all experienced the opposite—working with someone with plenty of smarts but a terrible attitude or someone who is friendly but never seems to do what needs to get done.

And having the right teammates isn't just about having more fun. It can be the difference between success and failure. Research shows that 23 percent of small businesses fail because they don't have the right team.[17] To make Collaboration work well, we need people who are a match in all three dimensions of the mind. When a person is constantly improving their cognitive skills, possesses a confident affect that fits your team, and has the conative strengths needed to fill the role, you know you've found the perfect fit.

Understanding the strengths of the people in our lives helps us shortcut the process and effectively choose when we should be working together and when we should work independently. If we remain aware of our strengths and the strengths of others, we can avoid making our strengths an imposing force and minimize conflict.

One father-son business partnership discovered that most of their problems in transitioning ownership happened because they didn't understand how their different strengths drove the way they took action, and how those differences would drive changes as the son stepped into the leadership role.

Their plan had been to bring the son in from his role at a similar real estate company, work closely with the father for a few years, and eventually have the son take over. The son was an Initiating Fact Finder (7-10) and a Preventative Quick Start (1-3), while the father's strengths sat at the other end of the continuum in both areas. That could be a great combination, with their strengths complementing each other, leading to higher performance for each.

But that's not what happened. Instead, the father expected his son to operate the same way he, the father, did. After all, the dad had built a successful business using these methods. The son tried to do it Dad's way. He really wanted to follow his father's pattern and earn his dad's respect. Unfortunately, reality didn't unfold according to plan.

After some initial success at the firm, fueled by his excitement about the opportunity, signs of conflict started appearing. Counter to ageist stereotypes, it was the "old guy" who naturally leaped at the chance provided by new leadership to try new things in the business. The son struggled to keep up with all the changes. He started pressing his dad to justify the new initiatives with data and projections. Because Dad lacked the information, the son quickly killed even promising ideas. Dad not only got frustrated, but he also started to lose confidence in his son's ability.

This struggle could have been avoided if they had begun the transition with clarity about the other person's strengths and understood how they could capitalize on their differences.

Clear communication and careful listening can minimize the dissonance and maximize conflict resolution between you and your collaborators. Understanding each other's conative traits will help immensely as you iron out problems and keep working in harmony.

Another key to resolution is to return to the three dimensions of the mind. Which part is the conflict rooted in? Does one person's experience or lack of knowledge lead to frustration? Or perhaps it's a personality conflict—someone's feelings or values need to be addressed. If it's neither of those, it's probably conative. Maybe you're just not on the same page because you approach problem solving in different ways.

The beauty of learning your own strengths and knowing the strengths of others is the way it empowers you to strategically choose who to work with on different projects. Two members of our Kolbe Corp team work particularly well together when they give presentations. Eric is an Initiating Quick Start. Even *he* doesn't know what might come out of his mouth when he's in front of a group. The person he works with on these presentations is an Initiating Follow Thru. Nicole is a natural at organizing information into a beautiful and effective slide deck. They work well together because Eric brings the sizzle of spontaneity to the presentation, while Nicole makes sure all the most important points get discussed. As a team, they get the best possible outcome that neither would have accomplished independently or if they chose to work with someone just like themselves.

Eric Herrera Kolbe A™ Result				Nicole Loucks Kolbe A™ Result			
Fact Finder	Follow Thru	Quick Start	Implementor	Fact Finder	Follow Thru	Quick Start	Implementor
			2			2	
	3						4
5				5			
					8		
		9					

There will always be opportunities to go solo. Some projects require a more independent approach. Plus, we have to recognize that even the greatest collaborators can drive each other crazy because their approaches are so different. This means we back off and work alone for a time and bring our creativity together again when appropriate.

Complement or Clone

Leaders need a team to grow their business, and relationally, we'll always have opportunities to expand our reach. But to truly succeed, adding people to your team, whether personally or professionally, has to be very intentional. Using a "we can train anyone" philosophy gives you as much of an edge as training a lineman to play quarterback.

Knowing and embracing your own strengths means you can begin to surround yourself with people who will help you accomplish your goals in the most effective and efficient way. It empowers you to ask, "Do I need someone who works the same way I do, or do I need someone who works differently?" This edge allows you to be strategic as you choose the best collaborators for a given situation or project.

Have you ever thought to yourself, "I really need a clone because there just isn't enough of me to get all of this done?" Some problems or projects require someone who is a conative copy of you. Working with them can minimize friction when your workload has grown past your capacity and you need someone to accomplish things the way you do. However, in any other circumstance, you won't be as productive. An entire team of clones will hold you back.

The most successful collaborative teams are filled with complements. Having people with different problem-solving approaches brings balance and perspective. As with the example of Eric and Nicole, finding a complement to your own strengths means together, you can accomplish marvelous things. The key to making these relationships work is recognizing the differences each of you brings to the table and making sure the rest of the team knows each other's MOs and how to leverage them. When you understand your strengths as well as the strengths of your team members, you'll be better prepared to Collaborate effectively and avoid the actions that will drive them crazy.

David's Story

As someone who enjoys doing research, sharing context, and accounting for many possible scenarios, I sometimes find myself adding complexity where it isn't needed. Even when I know it isn't helpful, I ask more questions. Fortunately, I have a solution to this problem that doesn't include forcing myself to operate in a way that drains my energy. My solution is to collaborate with Amy. She naturally simplifies. She pushes back when my need for information and explanation slows down decision making past the point of usefulness.

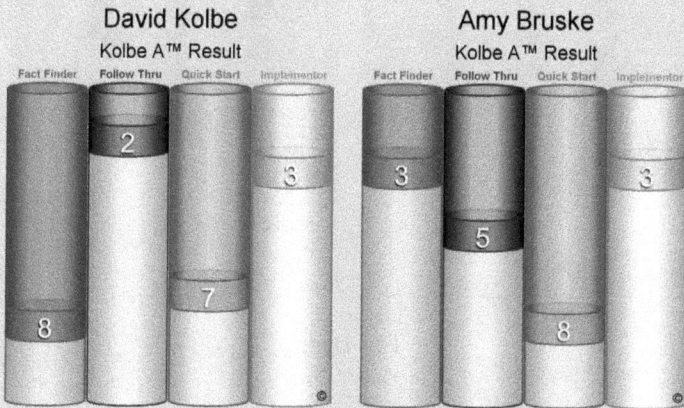

We've learned how to work together, trusting each other to use our strengths. In Fact Finder, we're pretty different, so we complement each other. We're similar in other respects, though, and I love that we get to work together in that way too. We both brainstorm new ideas and push to try out new concepts. Those sessions usually end up with us picking a couple of initiatives to bring to the expanded team to more fully flesh out.

Another great example of this is our client, Angelique Rewers, who figured this out the hard way. She and her husband, Mike, are on opposite ends of the Quick Start continuum, and he was not cut out to be her brainstorming partner. She frustrated him with all her unfiltered ideas, but he was brilliant as the CFO. She found a clone in Phil Dyer. Together, they would brainstorm possibilities until they had something concrete to bring to Mike. Then, he would analyze the risk factors, and together, they would decide what to pursue.

Angelique Rewers
Kolbe A™ Result

Mike Thompson
Kolbe A™ Result

Phil Dyer
Kolbe A™ Result

Conative Communication

A critical part of Collaboration is communication. Though you probably learned to talk when you were a toddler, effective expression takes more than a few words and an attitude. Emotion drives the desire to communicate, while thoughts provide the content. However, your conative instincts decide how the conversation plays out. The way you Initiate Action determines a significant part of your natural communication style, and understanding your own natural methods is critical. We tend to communicate with others based on our own needs and strengths. If you find people challenging to work with, it may be they are conatively different from you and communicate based on their own strengths.

FACT FINDER COMMUNICATION (7–10)

Keywords: researched, proven, specific

Tips when communicating:

- Be prepared with details
- Discuss priorities
- Allow for questions

FOLLOW THRU COMMUNICATION (7–10)

Keywords: process, system, schedule

Tips when communicating:

- Present thoughts in a sequential manner
- Describe how it fits in the plan
- Use charts, checklists, timelines

QUICK START COMMUNICATION (7–10)
Keywords: new, unique, challenge
Tips when communicating:

- Bring options
- Create a sense of urgency
- Allow for brainstorming

IMPLEMENTOR COMMUNICATION (7–10)
Keywords: quality, concrete, tools
Tips when communicating:

- Show (using props or models) vs. tell
- Physically demonstrate your point
- Communicate face-to-face

This was very true for our clients, Jerry Lujan and his daughter, Kelley. These conative opposites became so frustrated with each other one day that they both stopped and just started laughing. Fortunately, the two understood their strengths. Jerry realized Kelley was miserable when he operated in his zone and vice versa.

Jerry Lujan
Kolbe A™ Result

Kelley Lujan
Kolbe A™ Result

Kelley's natural way of communicating included sharing all the details and step-by-step processes for a project. However, before she could finish, Jerry would cut her off, and Kelley didn't do well with interruptions. Conversely, when Jerry felt inspired, he stopped in to bounce new ideas off Kelley even if she was in the middle of something, and she cut him off because she was trying to finish up with his previous brilliant idea. In order to communicate more effectively and save their relationship, they learned to set aside time specifically for Kelley to ask questions and Jerry to brainstorm. Afterward, they would go their own ways.

This has done wonders for their business and their relationship. And their business, ELEVATION180, has incorporated an understanding of conative strengths into their own "5 C's of Teamwork" model, which focuses on culture, clarity, commitment, collaboration, and communication.

Being the Best Teammate You Can Be

A good teammate contributes the best of themselves while letting all their team members shine. If everyone in your circle understands their conative strengths, you can quickly move into high production mode; however, not all Collaboration is quite so easy.

Maybe you remember being assigned a project in high school, and with the assignment came the names of three people you didn't know well. Worse, the teacher formed the teams without a thought for conative strengths—and often little consideration for personalities and skill. Unfortunately, some workplaces form teams using an equally random method.

If you understand your conative strengths, you now have an edge. Instead of simply throwing out a task list and deciding who wants to do what, you can be specific about the types of strengths needed to complete the tasks. Your questions become, "Who naturally Initiates research?" or "Who will organize the schedule?" Making assignments based on MO is a key to effective collaboration. Better yet, individuals can volunteer for the part of the project that allows them to best use their strengths.

Additionally, by knowing your MO, you can give others tips on how to work with you. One activity we use to help people build respect and learn how to communicate better is to invite each person in the room to share "one tip for working with me." A second activity is to have them share with the group how they would finish this sentence: "When I'm stressed, I need . . . ." These two pieces of information can be instrumental in creating successful communication in collaborations and make them a little less messy.

It's your responsibility to describe your conative needs to your teammates. For example, if you're an Initiating Follow Thru, be sure to let the team know you work best when you have uninterrupted time daily to check things off your list. You may feel presumptuous the first few times you share tips to make you more productive; however, when those around you experience your enhanced performance, they'll be happy to accommodate—better yet, they may want to discover their own strengths to make the entire workplace flow more smoothly. This doesn't give us permission to impose our MO on others or focus on our strengths at the expense of the rest of the team; however, it gives coworkers and managers an opportunity to make the workplace as productive as possible.

Working with the freedom to truly be yourself and being the best teammate means working independently from time to time. Collaboration brings energy and impact to your project; however, if you find yourself in an excessive number of meetings or your production drops due to forced teamwork, feel free to push back. Every collaboration should be strategic and helpful. Don't forget that collaboration can extend to everyone in your network, including vendors, contractors, and alliances.

Embracing your strengths makes you a valuable asset. Working in a group where everyone understands, respects, and embraces the others' strengths elevates everyone. They reach heights that would be unattainable if they were each performing individually. Like a jazz ensemble, when everyone knows when and how to step forward and take their solo, and the leader has a sense of who should carry the tune, notes of chaos and cacophony become works of harmony and beauty.

Key Takeaways

1. Collaborating with others can improve results, but it works best when teammates know and recognize each other's strengths.

2. Sometimes, you need to work with someone with similar strengths, a clone, and sometimes you need input from someone with different approaches, a complement.

3. People have different communication needs. It's up to you to let others know how to best communicate with you.

Chapter Ten
The Beauty of Diversity (Building Successful Teams)

Human nature causes us to naturally seek clones and avoid conflict and turmoil even if we know diversity makes a more effective team—one that can get more done in less time, requires fewer financial and personnel resources, and gives everyone more opportunities to work in their zone.

Perhaps we need to remember the African proverb, "If you want to go fast, go alone. If you want to go far, go together." That's the power of Collaboration. And when you incorporate the knowledge of conative strengths into the collaborative mix, the possibilities grow exponentially.

But going further faster means letting go of the way we do things and looking at the bigger picture. You're going to get frustrated along the way. Sometimes, the road to success requires us to deal with conflict and frustration. To maximize your efforts, instead of searching for people who work like you, ask yourself, "What do I need to look for in a team of collaborators to get things done in an excellent fashion, even if they don't use my method?"

Exponential Creativity

Though we mentioned it before, it bears repeating. Each of the three Zones of Operation in the four Action Modes is a strength—all 12 of them. The more problem-solving methods team members cover, the better.

Having people with a variety of problem-solving methods means there's a greater likelihood that someone on the team will be naturally adept at handling almost any challenges that come up. In contrast, teams with people whose conative strengths are cloned are less able to adapt their approach as the need arises. Another key benefit of diverse teams is that they are better able to work together rather than unknowingly getting trapped in loops of unproductive activity. One red flag indicating this has happened is when you start scheduling meetings to talk about future meetings.

Unfortunately, many teams won't have all 12 strengths represented or have them distributed perfectly. Most of us have experienced things like long and ineffective meetings, failing to meet project deadlines, indecision, and internal conflict. These are often symptoms of an imbalance of conative strengths. Teams where nearly everyone asks questions and adds to complexity, with no one to cut through the flood of data and grab hold of the essential elements of the project, become problematic.

Using the lottery system when setting up your team can lead to disaster. When the team is created strategically, with an eye toward conative diversity, making sure as many problem-solving methods as possible are represented, the creative power of your team increases exponentially. It's much like the famous Clydesdale horses. Bred to pull plows and wagons, each of these gentle giants can pull approximately 6,000 pounds. Simple math tells us that together, the two should be able to pull 12,000 pounds; however, a pair can easily pull 18,000 pounds. That's some impressive horsepower!

When you build a team with diverse conative strengths, you have the same kind of power. One plus one equals three. In fact, instead of using addition, we get to use multiplication. You can triple or quadruple your creativity and productivity by working with one other person. If you add one or two more with complementary strengths, you can accomplish even more. Without the strengths, four plus four equals eight. With conation, the same two fours can give you the multiplied power of 16.

The Advantage of a Diverse Team

The idea that working with people whose strengths complement each other produces better results isn't wishful thinking. It's reality.

Early in her learning, Kathy Kolbe did extensive work with engineering teams. During her research, she discovered a formula for an ideal distribution of strengths that covered all three Zones of Operation, which she called Conative Synergy. As she worked with clients, she noticed that interactive teams with a wide blend of conative strengths seemed to do better than teams with people whose strengths were grouped together. We interviewed both team leaders and team members to find out why.

Kathy recognized that the most successful teams had people who Initiated Action, regardless of what method they used to do it, as well as a balanced number of people to Resist or push back against that Initiation when actions went too far. She also noted the critical nature of having energy from the middle of the continuum to bridge the differences between the ends.

After we developed this theory of Conative Synergy, research at the University of Arizona put it to the test. That work, done in the engineering school, corroborated our observations. It showed that project teams closer to the ideal mix of Kolbe A Index results outperformed teams with worse synergy scores. Since then, we've replicated these results with many other clients.

Diversity in the way people instinctively take action is the key to maximizing team performance. The multiplier effect it brings will enable you to expand the impact of your team's efforts. When you need to collaborate or work interdependently, diversity of strengths is imperative.

However, team dynamics change based on the strengths your team needs. Many groups, such as sales or accounting teams, are full of individual contributors who don't necessarily rely on each other to accomplish their goals. Understanding the level of collaboration needed on your team will help determine how to work together successfully.

At Kolbe Corp, we use our formula for the ideal distribution of strengths to coach teams. When we see an imbalance of strengths, we can predict what kinds of situations might cause that particular team to get stuck or struggle.

Without someone who naturally pays attention to detail, they miss key deliverables. Too many of these Initiating Fact Finders cause analysis paralysis to stall the project. And a lack of those who bridge the gap means communication gets lost in every mode.

One product development team we worked with saw 80 percent of their team do their best work when they were given time to research and strategize the options for their next product. This team was heavy in 7–10s in Fact Finder. With no members on the other end of the continuum to push back against this Initiating strength, the team often found itself stuck in analysis paralysis. They never had enough information to satisfy the level of detail they needed to make a decision, so they consistently missed deadlines. After we raised their awareness of the way their team dynamics played out, they employed new strategies for collaboration and decision making allowing them to move forward more effectively.

In addition to an imbalance within an Action Mode, the lack of a particular strength can be just as problematic. Kolbe Corp has been invited to help product development teams without the natural drive to create new products and small businesses that began to stagnate after the founding generation of innovators retired and were replaced by teams who naturally resisted change. In each instance, the lack of diversity kept the business from reaching its full potential.

Basketball teams can be a good example of this principle in action. On many teams, the point guards run the plays and set the pace. If the point guard is an Initiating Follow Thru, you'll see them lead by executing according to the game plan, following a predetermined pace. The challenge arises when the plan starts to break down—the pass gets tipped or players aren't where they are supposed to be. Someone needs to adapt and execute without a plan, which requires a different strength. If the team is fortunate enough to have someone else who instinctively adapts to fluid situations and improvises solutions, you'll probably see that person step up and take over when the original play loses momentum. Those chaotic situations give this second player an opportunity to thrive, and their diverse strengths help the team win.

We've seen this dynamic work at the elite professional level when we helped the NBA's Phoenix Suns identify the conative strengths of potential draft picks and watched as those picks integrated with the players already on the team. And we've also seen the same dynamic play out watching and coaching our own kids in youth and high school sports.

Most people don't associate sports teams with conative diversity, but any group of people who need to create and execute a plan and deal with the chaos that comes when the plan falls apart requires members with diverse methods of action. More teams need to adopt the approach of high-performing professional basketball and soccer teams and give their members the confidence and autonomy to flow freely and move strategically without having the coach direct their every step.

When each person on your team recognizes and naturally moves in their strengths, projects can be completed as seamlessly as a basketball team taking the ball down the court and putting it through the hoop. Just like every guard knows their strength, and each forward moves into the right position to be ready when the pass comes their way, a team that moves in their strengths without waiting for permission and understands the strengths of their teammates will play well and create an amazing environment to work in.

It's also important to note the vital role the coach plays in this team setting. A strengths-focused coach knows how and when to encourage and give them a pat on the back. This coach realizes he cannot tell the Initiating Quick Start, "For 70 percent of the game, you're going to be less important because we have a plan to follow." That's demoralizing. However, if he goes to that same player and says, "You're my go-to when the game is on the line. Watch the clock because when we're down to the last few seconds or the game goes haywire, I'm counting on you to create some magic."

By understanding and celebrating players' strengths, the coach avoids egos getting involved. When everyone feels like they can contribute, it eliminates competition within the team. The stars on the court don't waste time and energy trying to imitate a style that will take them out of their zone.

In our experience, when a team is conatively diverse, projects cross the finish line with ease. With each person working in their own strengths zone, the process feels effortless. Procrastination is diminished because they thrive as they carry out their part of the project. And when everyone knows they won't be stuck working against their grain, engagement goes up and stress levels go down.

A great example of this was when we worked with about a dozen teams at Eastman Chemical. They were working on a multi-year, multi-million-dollar project. Before they began, they asked us to assess each team's potential success based on their Kolbe Index scores and predict how they would perform. Our prediction was so accurate that the head of technology raved about how knowing conative strengths and understanding how to create a diverse team was a major factor in their project's success. In fact, this project was acclaimed in the industry as a benchmark for similar global IT projects and was the first to come in on time and on budget in North America.

Do You Play Chess or Checkers?

Whether you're building your business or managing an existing team, knowing everyone's conative strengths helps you move people into the right position. You definitely don't want to set someone up for failure. Admittedly, collaboration and building a team can take time and energy; however, when you put people in positions that best suit their conative traits at the beginning, you won't have to repeat the process often. This focus on strengths is how you can get more done in less time and achieve more with fewer people. A quote by Marcus Buckingham puts the challenge in perspective: "Mediocre managers play checkers, assuming everyone is the same. Great managers play chess, acknowledging that everyone is unique."

Checkers is an easy game to teach young people. Every piece stays on the black squares. They all move exactly the same way—toward their opponent until they reach the other end of the board. Each clone, whether red or black, serves the same purpose. The only deviation those identical flat round pieces ever experience is being allowed to jump their opponent.

Unfortunately, most managers look at their employees as pieces on a checkerboard, and the team picks up that mindset, carrying it like a ball and chain. They feel stuck doing things in cookie-cutter ways that aren't a good fit for them.

Chess takes significantly more finesse. Every piece navigates the board according to different rules. All have unique capabilities. Each move requires a big-picture strategy. And while the queen seems to be the most powerful because she can go anywhere, often the knight offers the most advantageous move.

We encourage business leaders to look at conative strengths like the many options on a chess board. The people within your organization can't be swapped and traded like checkers. When you have to replace someone or integrate a new team member, your chances of winning the game increase exponentially when you use a chess-like strategy. Ask, "Which person's strengths will give us the biggest advantage three moves from now?"

At the same time, we believe that individuals need to look at themselves as chess pieces. Just because you have the capabilities to take over another person's tasks while they're unavailable doesn't mean that will be the most strategic move for you or the company.

People forced to work against their grain for long periods face burnout and illness, and their stress easily infects other members of the team. The effects of allowing team members to continue outside their strengths for extended periods can be as devastating as letting someone with the flu remain in the middle of a room full of healthy people. There's a direct correlation between constantly working contrary to conative strengths and employee turnover. A great leader can avoid many of these common problems.

Our client, EOS Worldwide, understands this and has incorporated Kolbe results into its LMA® (Leadership + Management = Accountability) process with all leaders. Their leader, Kelly Knight, says, "We consider the conative strengths of each person when deciding the frequency and structure of regular check-in meetings and quarterly conversations. If someone is an Initiating Quick Start, for example, we'll have shorter, more frequent check-ins. But if the person needs a lot of detail as an Initiating Fact Finder, we schedule longer weekly meetings so they have an opportunity to ask all of their questions. So, it's hugely helpful to have people in the right seat, not just for where we are right now but for where we're going."

When each person begins to see themselves as uniquely equipped with strengths like the pieces on a chess board, we'll be able to increase productivity as well as joy and peace in the workplace. Knowing the strengths of the team members allows a leader to look at the multiple gifts in the room and predict the parts of the project that will slow the group down and when they can expect to make great headway. They can make good decisions about when to bring in new team members and when to ask some to sit out a project. It will be up to the leader to set the tone. Leaders must know and work in their own strengths and then strategically position each team member according to their innate abilities. Otherwise, people will feel limited, and you'll be left with a board of pawns who could be kings and queens with the right direction.

You must make sure the entire team understands that their strengths and level of effort, rather than seniority or position, determine value in each situation or phase of the project. And much like a rare coin, if you have only one person with any particular strength, you have to treat that person as precious and make sure their voice is heard. If you have a team of six, and four of them are 1–3s in Quick Start while only Julie is an Initiating Quick Start, it's up to you, as the leader, to stand up and tell the team, "Do you know who is the most needed person on this team right now? The most critical person is Julie. I know she's a junior member and has the least seniority, but she's also the only one on the team who will be willing to take risks and try new things. We have to be very careful that we don't drown her out or dismiss her ideas because she's going to have random inspiration that may require big changes. With four Stabilizers on our team, it will be easy for us to shut her down. So, we need to be aware of that until we can find another Initiating Quick Starts to join us."

When you're adding to your team or hiring, beware. People tend to hire like-minded individuals. And while sharing similar values is important, without the insight that comes from understanding the conative part of the mind, you can easily end up with a team of clones without many complements. Those who do have diverse strengths will move on or be let go because frustration will build when expectations are based on their approach to problem solving rather than results.

Using conative strengths as a basis for hiring, firing, and moving people into new positions will give your organization a huge advantage. Employees who have permission to truly be themselves work more efficiently, and turnover rates in those workplaces plummet. At Kolbe Corp, we start by finding people who share our values and the values of the company. Then, we look for individuals whose innate strengths give them an advantage in the tasks we need to get done using the Kolbe RightFit™ system.[18] When people are in the right role and the team has a diverse set of strengths, you set your organization up for success. We should note that it's imperative to first analyze the conative demands of a job using a proven process, not make unsubstantiated assumptions, so you're able to accurately predict which Kolbe results are the right fit and will successfully predict successful job performance.

Key Takeaways

1. Teams with a diversity of instinctive strengths at the table will accomplish more in less time using fewer resources.

2. Each team member has a unique set of strengths—there are no "cookie-cutter" employees.

3. Leaders need to be aware of and familiar with the strengths of each person on their team in order to strategically combine them to achieve the multiplier effect.

Chapter Eleven

Developing a Strengths-Based Culture

If you want to create an environment with more engagement and less turnover, the entire culture of the organization must place a high value on strengths. You can't just pay it lip service. We've seen this happen in countless organizations. Some companies, even professional sports teams, have noble values emblazoned on the walls but don't actually put them into practice.

Performance and productivity hit peak levels when conative strengths become more than just individualized results or a list of numbers you refer to when assigning a project. To reach those heights, leaders must focus on sharing their vision of an excellent end result and leave the methods of achieving it to the individual. Allowing employees to operate in their most natural and productive ways with clear deliverables and deadlines sets everyone up for success.

A strengths-based culture uses conative strengths as a catalyst for everything but achieves high-level sustainable performance by balancing freedom and accountability. Everything we discussed earlier regarding individual success and the importance of the Three C's also applies to teams and organizations.

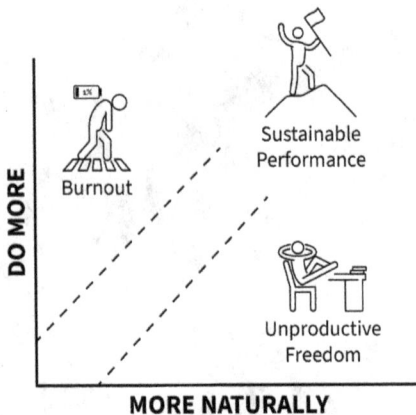

Leaders who push for results at any price risk burning out their best people. The most committed employees will rise to the challenge and give you their very best effort. Sadly, leaders with that press-for-more mindset won't realize the toll it takes on their people until it's too late. When output and increased quotas become the primary focus, you develop a do-more-at-all-costs culture, which is not sustainable.

While micromanaging and forcing people to do things your way doesn't work in the long run, the reverse situation won't work well either. A company that gives their people too much freedom to do their own thing in their own way without accountability for results won't achieve their goals any better than the do-more culture. This mindset will also eventually fail. Employees will be well-aligned to their jobs and may even be happy with them, but their time and energy will lack purpose and direction.

A thriving culture focused on strengths and Collaboration becomes self-sustaining. The Three C's allow it to operate with purpose. We see high levels of trust in these organizations because each person knows who to count on for what. People are engaged and comfortable relying on others and asking for help. Because they have the freedom to work in their strengths, they feel seen and heard, and they know their contributions are valued. A strengths-based culture creates an environment where self-starters blossom and flourish. These organizations optimize onboarding and require less managerial oversight.

Less Ego, More Instincts

We've all heard the jokes. "Do you think his ego will fit through the door?" "Can her ego handle someone else taking over?" All kidding aside, no one enjoys dealing with an egoist, especially at the office. Despite the fact these folks come across larger than life, their behavior reflects their lack of confidence.

One of our favorite outcomes from a strengths-based culture is a change in attitude and perspective, along with the lack of ego at home and in the workplace. People stop believing that their way of getting things done is the right way and start valuing the contributions made by others. As people understand how they're wired, they begin to sense their value and don't feel they need to be good at everything. Working in their strengths creates wins, and success increases confidence. Though it might take some time, the reinforcement that comes from the freedom to be yourself eventually removes the feeling that you need to cover all the bases yourself.

Confidence and a damaged ego cannot coexist. So, with ego out of the way, respect grows—respect for self and others. New leaders emerge because as people work in their natural instincts, those who once sat back quietly begin to step up when they see places where their strengths would help the group. At some point, every person on the team takes the lead as their MO becomes most useful in the moment.

An instincts-based team anticipates gaps and predicts outcomes by reviewing the strengths of their crew. They use missing traits as the measure to recruit coworkers for their project, and individuals aren't afraid someone will think poorly of them if they offer to remove themselves when the team seems heavy in their Initiating zone.

Playing to the strengths of all three parts of the mind gives us an amazing edge. Increased productivity and freedom are just the beginning. You'll be awestruck at the numerous benefits found in taking advantage of your strengths and the innate abilities of those around you.

Tapping into a strength-based mentality and prioritizing strengths as a lifestyle within our families, organizations, and workplaces makes life more enjoyable. When people have permission to turn down positions and tasks that fall outside their strengths, they'll get excited because they can Do More, More Naturally.

Key Takeaways

1. Doing More, More Naturally isn't just for individuals and their teams; it can make a big difference in the culture of a whole company.

2. It's important to find the balance between pushing for results and giving people the freedom to achieve those goals according to their strengths.

3. Building a strengths-based culture requires capitalizing on all three parts of the mind.

Chapter Twelve
Tag, You're It!

Learning to Do More, More Naturally may be the greatest gift you ever give yourself. In fact, when you make the decision to work in alignment with your natural strengths, it not only benefits you—the ripple effect never ends. It's easier than you think. It starts with applying the Three C's.

1. **Get Clarity**: Dive deep until you know and embrace your innate strengths. Understand that this instinctive way you take action is your superpower. It's a strength you should work with, celebrate, and combine with the strengths of others to make your life and the world a better place. By gaining clarity about your conative strengths, you'll be better positioned to make effective use of your action-taking energy.

2. **Commit Wisely**: Develop the skills and techniques that allow you to focus your energy on your priorities. Doing so will build well-earned confidence in your strengths as well as help you tap into what works for you and tune out the unhelpful advice and admonitions that deplete your energy.

3. **Collaborate Effectively**: Learn to leverage the strengths of others and be strategic about who you work with and when. Building a culture based on individuals' instinctive strengths will improve communication, reduce conflict, and help you achieve more using fewer resources.

But don't stop there. We know that the more people discover their instincts, the better off the world will be. We are all connected to each other. If we develop ourselves without ever looking to help others do the same, we won't move forward as a whole, whether that's as a family, a local community, a country, or a world.

Being a leader in a company or work environment isn't the only, or even necessarily the most important, way you can influence the world. We all have the ability to affect others. If you're a parent or adult of influence in the lives of kids, we hope you'll take the principles outlined in earlier chapters and help those kids discover their own instinctive strengths. Show them how they can accomplish great things by using those strengths to pursue their interests.

We need to remember that we should teach kids our values and be a guide helping them learn how they naturally take action. Trying to make a child use our unique approach won't help when our approach doesn't fit their strengths. Instead, that stokes frustration, guilt, and sometimes resentment.

You also influence the other adults you know and interact with. When they see you Doing More, More Naturally, they'll want to know how you did that. Please take the time to tell them, but don't tell them just what works for you. Most of them will have different strengths, so the best way to help them unlock the same ability is to show them how to gain clarity around their own strengths.

The great thing is this isn't a zero sum game. When the people around us have the joy of using their strengths and accomplishing more, it actually makes it easier for us to do the same. And there's a benefit that happens almost as a side effect. When we understand at a fundamental level that none of us have all the skills and strengths needed to accomplish great things, we learn to respect and value the gifts of others. We don't just tolerate who other people are, we respect, appreciate, and celebrate the way they operate because it makes us all richer.

We've helped millions of people start down this path, but that isn't enough. We need millions more, maybe tens of millions more, to learn to trust their own instincts and empower others to do the same to have a lasting, measurable impact on our world. It's our mission to make that happen. By reading this book, you now know our secret to effortless success—a secret we want you to tell everyone. We've passed along to you the knowledge and gift of freedom that Kathy passed to us, so now it's your turn to set someone free. As Kathy would say, "Tag! You're It!"

Chapter Thirteen
Taking Action

Chapter Thirteen
Taking Action

We've written this book to provide a new understanding and mindset shift that will allow you to Do More, More Naturally. We know it also helps to use tools and solutions to turn that understanding into concrete progress toward achieving your goals.

One of our most popular reports is Comparisons: A to A™. Here's an example of how we've used it to improve our own collaboration:

David's Story

The head of technology at Kolbe Corp, James, is at the opposite end of the Follow Thru spectrum from me in terms of how we organize, deal with plans, and structure. We've accomplished a lot together over more than 25 years and know each other well, but sometimes we both need reminders about what to do and not do, to keep that partnership thriving. Our Kolbe Comparisons: A to A Report reminds me that I'll frustrate James if I expect him to take shortcuts or leave projects unfinished so he can switch to what I think are more important priorities. And the report reminds him that he takes me out of my game if he limits my ability to be open ended and change plans when I see that things aren't working.

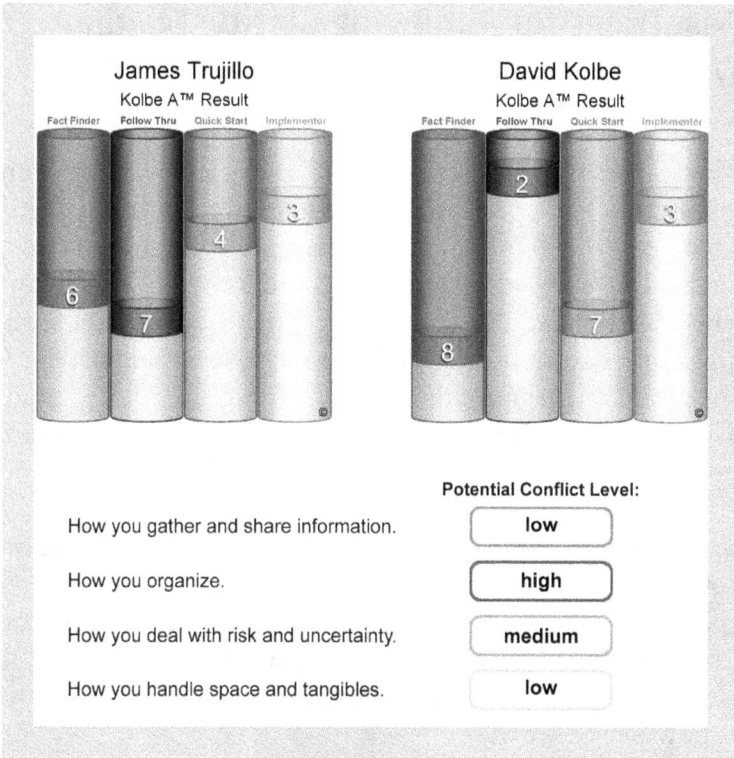

James Trujillo
Kolbe A™ Result

Fact Finder | Follow Thru | Quick Start | Implementor

David Kolbe
Kolbe A™ Result

Fact Finder | Follow Thru | Quick Start | Implementor

	Potential Conflict Level:
How you gather and share information.	low
How you organize.	high
How you deal with risk and uncertainty.	medium
How you handle space and tangibles.	low

The Comparisons: A to A is just one of the numerous resources that we've created for our clients to help them Do More, More Naturally. Many of these tools are designed so you can use them on your own, but you'll experience even greater impact if you work with a Kolbe Certified™ Consultant. They can act as a coach for individuals or a consultant to your organization by applying their expertise to your particular situation. You can find a Kolbe Certified Consultant to be a partner in this process at Kolbe.com/FindaConsultant.

Resources for Achieving Clarity, Making Wise Commitments, and Successful Collaboration

The first step in this journey is to gain clarity about your instinctive strengths by taking the Kolbe A Index. The Kolbe A is the foundation for all our products and services. People move ahead by leaps and bounds when they know who they are and can show the people they interact with how they naturally take action and solve problems. And once someone learns this about themself, they understand why it's our mission for everyone to know and understand their instinctive strengths.

The Kolbe A Index measures a person's instinctive way of doing things and the result is called their MO (method of operation). It is the only validated assessment that measures a person's conative strengths (not their IQ or personality). Unlike any other assessments or quizzes, Kolbe gets directly at how people execute.

Activate Your A™ Discovery Course – This self-paced, online course provides an overview of Kolbe theory, including the three Parts of the Mind, the three C's to success, and how a person's Kolbe result compares to some other assessments they've taken. It's the best way for them to start using their instinctive strengths to get more done, more naturally. For Activate Your A™ Solutions visit Kolbe. com/ActivateYourA.

Activate Your A™ Guide – This workbook is a powerful companion guide to the Kolbe A™ Index. The three sections will take a person through highlighted portions of their Kolbe A Index result and specific applications for productivity, stress, and communication. With 20+ fully-customized activities to enhance their understanding and appreciation of instinctive strengths, it's a perfect way to get more out of your Kolbe Index results.

Kolbe Coaching Reports – Based on a person's Kolbe A result, these detail the best ways to manage and motivate someone by tapping into their instinctive talents. Designed especially for managers and supervisors, each report is customized for a specific person's Kolbe A Index result and offers individualized strategies for improving performance.

Kolbe Plus Workshop – This workshop is designed to deepen your understanding of your Kolbe A™ Index result and how the Kolbe Theory impacts team dynamics. Participants gain hands-on experience with tools and strategies to maximize personal productivity, identify and reduce job-related stress, and build stronger teams. Led by expert consultants, this interactive session empowers leaders to start the journey towards Doing More, More Naturally. For more information visit Kolbe.com/KolbePlus.

Job Alignment Solutions include assessments (Kolbe B™ and C™ Indexes), which identify job-holder perceptions and supervisor expectations. A series of Comparisons reports analyzes them and provides tips and tricks for reducing stress and improving performance and job satisfaction.

The Kolbe Comparisons: A to A™ is an operating manual for those who collaborate at work. It helps two people better understand each other's Kolbe Strengths™, how they can work together more productively, and triggers to avoid. It provides an analysis of conative strengths and potential for conative stress between two people with a customized report that outlines tips designed for those two people to increase their effectiveness and meaningful communication.

Kolbe TeamSuccess® Solutions – Customized seminars and reports designed to maximize teamwork and strategically combine talents. These offer a variety of options for length and specific content and focus on how to improve communication and collaboration among team members, eliminate frustrating, long, and unproductive meetings, and create a culture of respect, accountability, and performance.

Perfect for team building and retreats, these dynamic sessions provide an engaging and interactive way to explore the workings of specific teams within a business. The workshop inventories instinctive talents that make up the actual—not just desired—culture. Participants learn ways to leverage these strengths, enabling them to work together consistently and effectively. Leaders are given diagnostic and prescriptive information to accelerate team productivity as well as tools to improve communication and clarify commitment levels.

Kolbe RightFit™ Hiring System – Kolbe Corp's statistically proven hiring process helps companies screen and select the best job applicants. It enables users to rate candidates based on the conative needs of the role. So, instead of guessing how well a prospective employee will perform, you can see whose natural strengths will line up well with a given job.

Once you've hired a candidate who is a good fit for a particular role, make sure that you onboard them effectively. Set them up for success by giving their manager a Coaching Report and providing a Comparisons: A to A between the new hire and their direct supervisor. As time goes by, adding in other role alignment and team reports will help everyone to work together better.

Kolbe Certification™ Seminar – Kolbe Certification is an immersive three- or four-day training program that provides organizational leaders, management consultants and professional coaches an in-depth understanding of the Kolbe System™ and foundational theory. This highly interactive learning experience covers the tools and knowledge needed to become an in-house or independent Kolbe specialist. For more information visit Kolbe.com/Certification.

Personal Applications

Our conative strengths aren't confined to our workplace. Any time you're engaged and striving, your strengths are in play. Kolbe offers applications with insights and advice for those personal situations and relationships that matter most to you.

Takes Two® compares a couple's conative strengths and uncovers the hidden factors that help your committed romantic relationship. This report includes tips for communication, household chores, finances, and vacations.

Most people don't realize that Kathy Kolbe began delving into the intricacies of conative strengths in 1975 by working with students to help them achieve their personal goals. She's long had a passion to understand children's creative processes and use that knowledge to propel them to success.

Kolbe Youth™ Index or **Student Aptitude™ Quiz** is similar to the Kolbe A™ Index but designed for young people starting at a 4th-grade reading level. Online results include an audio recording explaining they can use their instinctive strengths to be creative and solve problems. There are add-on reports available to help with stress and studying for and taking tests.

Kolbe Parent Guide™ – An easy-to-follow companion guide to the youth assessment that aids parents and care-givers in supporting their child's striving instincts. Parents learn how to recognize and honor their child's instinctive strengths so they can provide support with solving prob-lems, improving communication skills, and increasing the opportunity for personal success in school, extracurricular activities, social situations, and at home.

Amy's Story

My daughter understood her conative strengths before she turned seven thanks to her grandmother's observations. When she had to present a speech in first grade I asked if she wanted to practice in front of me. She replied, "Mom, you know I'm going to get up there and make it up." She already understood the way she was wired to create and act. Though she chose not to prepare for her speech the way her teacher expected, she had confidence that as long as she did her best and achieved an excellent result, we supported the way she took action.

The understanding our daughter gained growing up has helped her immensely as she chose a career and specialty. The secret was in her awareness of herself and her conative needs.

For more information about Kolbe Theory, products or services, please visit Kolbe.com or the Appendix.

Appendix

Following are details of the concepts and programs referenced throughout the book. This Appendix includes the materials and programs we provide in seminars and consulting for individuals and organizations.

Kathy Kolbe's definition of success: "Success is the freedom to be yourself."

In order to be free to be yourself, you need to maximize the potential of all three of your mental factors.

Kolbe Theory of Conation

Three Mental Factors/Parts of the Mind

Ancient philosophers and modern psychologists share the concept of a three-part mind with separate domains for thinking, feeling, and doing. The conative, or doing part, contains the striving instincts that drive a person's natural way of taking action, or modus operandi (MO). This is the unique set of innate strengths and talents every person has that remain unchanged from birth. Everyone has an equal amount of conative energy for engaging the thinking (cognitive) and feeling (affective) parts of the mind to produce purposeful action.

Conation

Conation is action derived from instinct, a purposeful mode of striving or volition. It is a conscious effort to carry out self-determined acts.

The Latin *conatus*, from which conation is derived, is defined as "any natural tendency, impulse, or directed effort."

Although ancient philosophers up through early 20th-century psychologists accepted conation, few concepts concerning it have survived unscathed from subsequent debates.

Three Zones of Operation in the Four Action Modes

There are three Zones of Operation in each of the four Action Modes measured on a unit scale of 1 to 10. Each utilizes equal amounts of mental energy for creative problem solving and decision making.

Initiating Actions: The first thing people do is take actions that tie to their most insistent Action Mode. It's the longest line on their Kolbe A Index result. People will Initiate Action through any of the Action Modes in which they have 7 to 10 units of conative energy (as shown on their Kolbe A Index result).

ReActions/Accommodate: Conative ReActions moderate responses. They are an instinctive way of accommodating both Initiating actions and the natural push back to them, CounterActions. People ReAct in any mode in which they have 4 to 6 units of conative energy. ReActions are just as powerful as Initiating actions.

CounterActions/Prevent: Conative CounterActions offer a counterpoint to the way action is being taken, provide the instinctive strength to Resist the way things are happening, and Prevent problems when there is too much energy to Initiate a particular type of action. People CounterAct in any mode in which they have 1 to 3 units of conative energy. Like ReActions, CounterActions are just as powerful as Initiating actions.

Fact Finder: The instinctive way we gather and share information.

Behavior ranges from gathering detailed information and documenting strategies to simplifying and clarifying options.

Operating Zone	Fact Finder Actions
Initiating (7–10)	Details, strategies, research
Accommodating (4–6)	Specifics, editing, assessing pros and cons
Preventing (1–3)	Analysis paralysis, or minutiae

Follow Thru: The instinctive way we organize and design.

Behavior ranges from being systematic and structured to being adaptable and flexible.

Operating Zone	Follow Thru Actions
Initiating (7–10)	Systems, procedures, design, order
Accommodating (4–6)	By adjusting to existing plans, maintaining classifications
Preventing (1–3)	Getting boxed in, being overly structured

Quick Start: The instinctive way we deal with risk and uncertainty.

Behavior ranges from driving change and innovation to stabilizing and preventing chaos.

Operating Zone	Quick Start Actions
Initiating (7–10)	Change, deadlines, uniqueness
Accommodating (4–6)	By mediating between the vision and the given, facilitating change
Preventing (1–3)	Chaos, minimizing risk

Implementor: The instinctive way we handle space and tangibles.

Behavior ranges from making things more concrete by building solutions to being more abstract by imagining a solution.

Operating Zone	Implementor Actions
Initiating (7–10)	Demonstrations, physical solutions
Accommodating (4–6)	By using machinery or implements for either tangible or intangible effort
Preventing (1–3)	Need for tangible evidence, overbuilt solutions

Kathy Kolbe's 5 Rules for Trusting Your Instincts

1. **Act—Before You Think.** Do what you never thought you could.

   When you Act—Before You Think, it keeps you from rationalizing your way out of making a decision. Don't stop and consider what you should do; instead, trust your instincts. Too often people fear looking foolish and, as a result, end up being victims. They don't run out of the church when their gut tells them not to say, "I do." Or they don't run for cover before disaster strikes.

2. **Self-Provoke.** Get where you want to go.

   Goad yourself to Initiate the action you desire. Some ways to self-provoke are:

   - Inspire your own achievements
   - Direct your energies
   - Push yourself into action
   - Make what you want to happen, happen
   - Ignite your own instincts
   - Create your own opportunities

3. **Commit—But to Very Little.** Target your top priorities.

   You need to make commitments, but if you commit to too many things at one time, your instincts will get whiplash. They'll be thrust back and forth among so many priorities that you'll find it difficult to concentrate on what matters most.

We recommend commitment contracts between people, both at work and at home. It's a process that lays out the use of time and mental energy so both parties can see the logic of how they're allocated. It brings reality into conversations that can become strictly emotional and accusatory.

4. **Be Obstinate—in Overcoming Obstacles.** Stick with your instincts.

Being obstinate includes tenacity, perseverance, and dogged resolution, having a ruling passion, being willful, and acting with determination.

If you don't overcome the obstacles that keep you from having the freedom to act on instinct, you will never live up to your potential.

5. **Do Nothing—When Nothing Works.** Take charge of time-outs.

This is how you protect the use of your instinctive energy. It helps you shut off the energy leaks that go toward non-purposeful actions. It removes the mental clutter in your life.

For more information about Kolbe Theory, products or services, please visit Kolbe.com.

Endnotes

1. Clifton, Jim. *The Chairman's Blog.* "The World's Broken Workplace." June 13, 2017. https://news.gallup.com/opinion/chairman/212045/world-broken-workplace.aspx.

2. Morris, Kathy. *Zippia.* "Survey: 50% of People Hate Their Jobs—Here's why." February 13, 2022 https://www.zippia.com/advice/why-people-hate-their-jobs/.

3. Seltzer PhD, Leon F. *Psychology Today.* "How Do You Define Success?" July 7, 2021. https://www.psychologytoday.com/us/blog/evolution-the-self/202107/how-do-you-define-success.

4. Harrell, Eben. *Harvard Business Review.* "A Brief History of Personality Tests." March-April 2017. https://hbr.org/2017/03/a-brief-history-of-personality-tests.

5. "Conation." Accessed January 18, 2024. http://conation.org/theoryHumanInstinctsConation.html.

6. See Appendix for "Kathy Kolbe's 5 Rules for Trusting Your Instincts".

7. See Appendix for "Kathy Kolbe's 5 Rules for Trusting Your Instincts".

8. Schlosser, Kurt. *Geekwire.* "Fifty Shades of Mark Zuckerberg." January 26, 2016. https://www.geekwire.com/2016/mark-zuckerberg-grey-wardrobe/.

9. See Appendix for Kathy Kolbe's 5 Rules for Trusting Your Instincts.

10. Parren, Alexandria. *Sundried.* Accessed July 30, 2024. https://www.sundried.com/blogs/training/research-shows-43-of-people-expect-to-give-up-their-new-year-s-resolutions-by-february?currency=GBP.

11. See Appendix for "Kathy's 5 Rules for Trusting Your Instincts".

12. Gladwell, Malcolm. *The New Yorker.* "Complexity and the Ten-Thousand-Hour Rule." August 21, 2013.

https://www.newyorker.com/sports/sporting-scene/complexity-and-the-ten-thousand-hour-rule.

13 *Headspace.* "What is a flow state, and what are the benefits?" Accessed January 26, 2024. https://www.headspace.com/articles/flow-state.

14 Forleo, Marie. *CNBC Make It.* "Self-Made Millionaire." September 13, 2019. https://www.cnbc.com/2019/09/13/self-made-millionaire-how-to-increase-your-odds-of-success-by-42-percent-marie-forleo.html.

15 See Appendix for "Kathy Kolbe's 5 Rules for Trusting Your Instincts".

16 Godlewski, Nina. *Fundera.* "Small Business Revenue Statistics: Annual Sales and Earnings." January 23, 2023. https://www.fundera.com/resources/small-business-revenue-statistics.

17 McIntyre, Georgia. *Fundera.* "What Percentage of Small Businesses Fail?" November 20, 2020. https://www.fundera.com/blog/what-percentage-of-small-businesses-fail.

18 Kolbe RightFit™ software is used for this analysis.

Acknowledgements

This book went from idea to reality only because of the talent and support of many, many people. We mean what we say about collaboration and want to thank the people whose strengths and energy gave us the freedom to use our own strengths to create what you've read.

We especially want to thank our Kolbe Corp team, led by Christine Morrow, whose dedication and focus as both a project manager and editor were truly remarkable. We also appreciate the enthusiasm and contributions of our other teammates, including Toby Phillips, Stephanie Clergé, Eric Herrera, Nicole Loucks, James Trujillo, Carrie Reed, and Logan Mosier.

Thanks to those who read early versions and shared invaluable feedback: Craig Coppola, Giana Dimarco, Justin Brown, Trisha Howard, and Tristan Pelligrino.

We're so grateful to our clients, friends, and family who agreed to let their stories be examples to others in the book. Thank you for your generosity: Dan Sullivan, Babs Smith and Shannon Waller of Strategic Coach; Kelly Knight and Mark O'Donnell of EOS; Angelique Rewers, Mike Thompson and Phil Dyer of Boldhaus; Jerry and Kelley Lujan of ELEVATION180.

Huge thanks to the team at Igniting Souls, who were so supportive in helping us craft, complete, and bring this book to the world, in particular Kary Oberbrunner, Lynne Modranski, Ruthie Bult, and Sarah Grandstaff.

And finally, we want to thank Kathy Kolbe, both for the gift she's given the world in understanding their strengths, and the love and support she's given us as we continue the work she started.

David: I especially want to thank my wife Pam for her insight, patience, love, and strength in Follow Thru, and my kids, Grace, Jack, Anna, and Sophie, all of whose wit, discernment, and affection infuse me (and the world around them) with joy, purpose, and clarity.

Amy: To my husband Jim, thank you for your unwavering support and encouragement that enables me to do what I love. To my kids, CJ and Kate, you give me a greater sense of purpose and inspire me to make a difference in people's lives. And, to my dad, Will Rapp, thank you for always being my biggest fan.

About the Authors

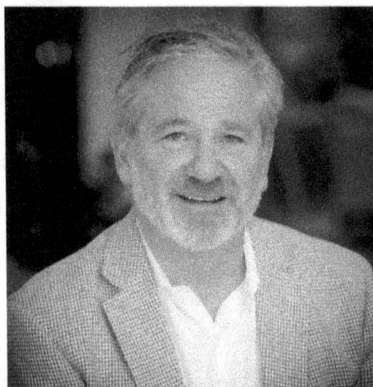

David Kolbe is transforming how the world understands human performance. He comes from a lineage of psychometric pioneers and is the CEO of Kolbe Corp, a company committed to helping people achieve what they care about most. David has lived and breathed the Kolbe Concept® and helped develop the original algorithm for the Kolbe A™ Index — the only proven tool to unlock instinctive strengths. He's passionate about helping people discover their strengths, reduce their stress, and find more joy at work and home. Top companies call David because he knows the secret to unleashing innovation and building teams that thrive, and has the scientific validation to back it up. David is known for his speeches and workshops that blend wit, interactivity and introspection. With a rich background in law and business, David has an exceptional knack for turning innovative ideas into profitable ventures. Before he joined Kolbe Corp, David was an attorney at a top Arizona law firm and a Legislative Director in Congress. He also holds a degree in economics from the Wharton School of Business. When he's not at work, you can find David skiing down a mountain, playing poker, or immersing himself in music. He calls Arizona home.

Amy Bruske has had a life-long obsession with human behavior, and she's on a quest to help driven people find the freedom to be themselves. Amy is the expert voice for real-world applications of the Kolbe Concept® — the authoritative theory for human instinct and performance. As President and an owner of Kolbe Corp, she spends her days advising Fortune 500 companies, top government agencies, and rapidly growing small businesses about how to Do More, More Naturally. Her innovative training programs and provocative speeches energize a global cohort of high-impact consultants and hundreds of teams each year. She partnered with renowned theorist Kathy Kolbe to author *Business is Business* — the groundbreaking family business guide. Amy never stops learning from others and has a keen eye for useful tips and best practices, which is why she commits extensive time to serving on boards such as the Arizona Hispanic Chamber of Commerce and joining organizations like the Women Presidents' Organization and the International Women's Forum. She serves as Chairman of the Board for the Center for Conative Abilities in Arizona, where she lives with her family. Outside the office, Amy is a true crime podcast enthusiast, a meditation and yoga devotee, and a fan of light-hearted TV shows.

KOLBE CORP

GET YOUR KOLBE RESULT TODAY!

PLUS, AN EXCLUSIVE OFFER

Kolbe.com/DoMoreBonus

CONNECT WITH AMY

Follow him on your favorite social media platforms today.

Kolbe.com/DoMoreBonus

THIS BOOK IS PROTECTED INTELLECTUAL PROPERTY

Instant IP™

The author of this book values Intellectual Property. The book you just read is protected by Instant IP™, a proprietary process, which integrates blockchain technology giving Intellectual Property "Global Protection." By creating a "Time-Stamped" smart contract that can never be tampered with or changed, we establish "First Use" that tracks back to the author.

Instant IP™ functions much like a Pre-Patent™ since it provides an immutable "First Use" of the Intellectual Property. This is achieved through our proprietary process of leveraging blockchain technology and smart contracts. As a result, proving "First Use" is simple through a global and verifiable smart contract. By protecting intellectual property with blockchain technology and smart contracts, we establish a "First to File" event.

Protected by Instant IP™

LEARN MORE AT INSTANTIP.TODAY

www.ingramcontent.com/pod-product-compliance
Lightning Source LLC
Chambersburg PA
CBHW070657190326
41458CB00053B/6915/J